Cambridge Elements

Elements in Magic
edited by
William Pooley
University of Bristol

GERALD GARDNER AND THE CREATION OF WICCA

John Callow
University of Suffolk

Shaftesbury Road, Cambridge CB2 8EA, United Kingdom

One Liberty Plaza, 20th Floor, New York, NY 10006, USA

477 Williamstown Road, Port Melbourne, VIC 3207, Australia

314–321, 3rd Floor, Plot 3, Splendor Forum, Jasola District Centre, New Delhi – 110025, India

103 Penang Road, #05–06/07, Visioncrest Commercial, Singapore 238467

Cambridge University Press is part of Cambridge University Press & Assessment, a department of the University of Cambridge.

We share the University's mission to contribute to society through the pursuit of education, learning and research at the highest international levels of excellence.

www.cambridge.org
Information on this title: www.cambridge.org/9781009713870

DOI: 10.1017/9781108956161

© John Callow 2025

This publication is in copyright. Subject to statutory exception and to the provisions of relevant collective licensing agreements, no reproduction of any part may take place without the written permission of Cambridge University Press & Assessment.

When citing this work, please include a reference to the DOI 10.1017/9781108956161

First published 2025

A catalogue record for this publication is available from the British Library

ISBN 978-1-009-71387-0 Hardback
ISBN 978-1-108-95838-7 Paperback
ISSN 2732-4087 (online)
ISSN 2732-4079 (print)

Cambridge University Press & Assessment has no responsibility for the persistence or accuracy of URLs for external or third-party internet websites referred to in this publication and does not guarantee that any content on such websites is, or will remain, accurate or appropriate.

For EU product safety concerns, contact us at Calle de José Abascal, 56, 1°, 28003 Madrid, Spain, or email eugpsr@cambridge.org

Gerald Gardner and the Creation of Wicca

Elements in Magic

DOI: 10.1017/9781108956161
First published online: October 2025

John Callow
University of Suffolk
Author for correspondence: John Callow, callow2001@hotmail.com

Abstract: Gerald Gardner (1884–1964) provided the central inspiration for Wicca, as a modern, revived, form of Pagan witchcraft. As such, his cultural and religious significance has grown exponentially over the 60 years since his death.
'A Rough Magic' re-evaluates the sources of Gardner's inspiration, redefines his early life within the context of colonial Malaya and the opium trade, and emphasises his vision and ability in fashioning an entirely new synthesis of magical beliefs drawn from both Eastern and Western traditions. In so doing, he stripped away the demonic elements of witchcraft and emphasised Wicca as a creative, mutable and undogmatic nature religion, serving as both fertility cult and a unique source of personal empowerment, that was capable of transforming the world.

Keywords: Wicca, Gerald Gardner, Witchcraft, Paganism, Magic

© John Callow 2025
ISBNs: 9781009713870 (HB), 9781108958387 (PB), 9781108956161 (OC)
ISSNs: 2732-4087 (online), 2732-4079 (print)

Contents

1 The Fool's Journey: Gerald Gardner and the Historians   1

2 The Magus and the Magic of the Tribe   9

3 The Magician: Studies in Praxis   19

4 The Sun and the Moon: Fashioning Wicca and Writing Witchcraft   30

5 The Tower: Witchcraft on the Isle of Man   40

6 The High Priestess: Feminising the New 'Old' Religion   53

7 The World: The Achievement of Modern Paganism   65

Bibliography   71

1 The Fool's Journey: Gerald Gardner and the Historians

The witch has always lived upon the margins. Penumbral and fleeting, her imprint barely registered within mainstream academia before the last decades of the twentieth century. Fear, dismissal, and derision had been her fate. The triumph of Cartesian thought in the West and the Enlightenment's emphasis upon empiricism and reason had served to physically remove the witch figure from the community, incarcerating her in the poorhouse, while banishing the idea of her to the nursery and the pages of the storybook. If the High Magic of ceremonial magicians, most notably centred around the Hermetic Order of the Golden Dawn, could appear as a cerebral and empowering off-shoot of the late Victorian esoteric revival, then, belief in the powers of the village witch, or 'cunning person', seemed both facile and risible: the expression of credulity and superstition.

Viewed from this perspective, the recovery and resurgence of a form of modern Paganism, that would come to be known as Wicca and took the feminised and feminist witch as its source of inspiration, might be seen to be a particularly unlikely and ill-starred project. That it succeeded and spread rapidly from its twin crucibles of Southern England and the Isle of Man crossing the Atlantic to North America, to emerge as a viable world religion, as coherent and as worthy of study and engagement as any other, was nothing short of remarkable and was largely due to the endeavours, vision, and restless promotion of one man: Gerald Gardner, the subject of this study.

Yet, before charting that rise it is necessary to acknowledge, in sifting the fact from the fantasy, that the sources for Gardner's life and the intellectual genesis of Wicca were, themselves, shaped – and often distorted – by the marginality of their practitioners and by the cursory dismissal of Pagan practices and spirituality, until very recently, by mainstream commentators. The difficulty in historicising Wicca (as understood by Gardner) stems from its nature and practice as an initiatory, coven-based, mystery religion. It was experiential and, therefore, highly personal and subjective, guided by the group egregore as opposed to a central doctrine. It was also constantly evolving, in terms of both its ritual content and philosophy, during Gardner's stewardship (from approximately 1948 to 1964). As a consequence, any attempt to try to set Wicca in aspic is doomed to failure, as its form and practice varied considerably over this period and between the different working groups (or covens) that he founded.

It is as well to acknowledge from the outset that a palpable tension exists between the requirements of an oath-bound, coven-based, nature religion and the desire of the historian or anthropologist to define, systematise, and to reveal both the lineaments and sinews of a hitherto hidden (and literally occult) form of comparative religion. This renders Wicca a particularly elusive quarry and one that requires a sensitive and nuanced approach resembling those taken in relation to indigenous religions and the Aboriginal 'dream time', as opposed to examinations of formally organised, faith based, systems, where the word – rather than the deed – informs and prescribes set doctrines and practices.

Just such a sympathetic and immersive approach was adopted by Tanya Luhrmann in her account of the workings of the Bricket Wood Coven in the 1980s (published as *Persuasions of the Witch's Craft* in 1989). This was a landmark study in social anthropology that sought, for an academic audience steeped in Western rationalism, to account for the resurgence of magical beliefs among a counterculture of intelligent, educated, urban, and urbane Londoners. For us, its significance lies in the fact that much of the primary research was conducted within a coven that traced its lineage directly back to Gerald Gardner and that it was the first scholarly account that treated Wicca as a serious field of enquiry. However, within this context it is notable that Gardner – having been described as 'a civil servant' who 'created' modern witchcraft – is thereafter relegated to the sidelines, appearing only in the guise of the absent subject.[1]

Thus, at the very moment when Wicca was poised to transform itself from a numerically small initiatory cult to a growing global religion, Gardner's role became tangential to a wider developmental narrative, while his personality was compressed within the confines of a job title implicitly laden with value judgements regarding social attitudes and class relationships, access to educational opportunities and a relationship to state power that have, ever since, been used to define him and to distort his life, career and contribution to the history of revived Paganism.

There were three main reasons for the formation and sustained promotion of this lacuna. The first was rooted in Gardner's own *modus operandi,* whereby, in promoting his vision of an enduring, underground fertility religion dating back as far as the Palaeolithic Age, he presented himself as a simple member of the 'witch cult', transmitting only those elements deemed necessary or permissible by the wider collective to the public sphere. This had the effect of foregrounding his image of the feminised witch, in the form of the High Priestess, and of creating an aura of mystery and timelessness about Wicca that helped to promote the idea of the new religion as being a remarkable survival from pre-history. However, it also served to diminish the impact of Gardner's creative vision, and personality, within Wicca, itself, as he became (by his own definition) a simple interlocutor for 'the witches'.

---

[1] T. M. Luhrmann, *Persuasions of the Witch's Craft: Ritual Magic in Contemporary England*, (London: Picador, 1989 rpt. 1994), p. 46.

The second turned upon gender. It was in no one's interest to place a man at the fount of goddess worship as it failed to fit either the paradigm that Gardner, himself, had established, in the 1950s, or the radical social and political priorities of the new wave of feminism, from the late 1960s through to the early 1980s. In this, Gardner was very much the victim of his own success. If he had not been able to find a pre-existing network of pagan priestesses and struggled, during his early years on the Isle of Man, to find any female adepts at all (hiring waitresses and locals to 'play' the part of aspiring witches for the media), then, he left behind him a coven structure that, through his promotion of intelligent, articulate, and media-friendly High Priestesses (such as Doreen Valiente, Monique Wilson, Lois Bourne, and Patricia Crowther), both appeared and functioned as a true matriarchy. Thus, the arrival of Wicca in the United States, in the early 1960s, caught the spirit of the age and rapidly outgrew its initial coven structure, based upon Long Island.

Over the course of the next two decades, the popularity of the North American movement was generated, in large measure, by scores of cheaply but vividly produced mass market accounts of modern witchcraft – delighting in such titles as *Ancient & Modern Witchcraft: The Truth About Witchcraft by a Witch High Priest!*, *A Cauldron of Witches*, and *The Witches Workbook. The Magick Grimoire of Lady Sheba* – that sat comfortably upon newsagents' shelves and purported to offer an insight into the deepest workings of contemporary witchcraft.[2] These exposes slipped under the radar of the academic community, and, as their selling points often depended upon the willingness of individuals to break coven-bound oaths to deliver the 'secrets of the Craft' to publishers and public, alike, the personalities of authors and their own claims to understanding of an underground 'tradition' eased-out any debt to Gardner and the, very recent, establishment of initiatory Wicca.

The third, and most damaging, reason for Gardner's relegation to the shadows came in the form of a scurrilous and self-serving attack upon his ideas and character penned by Charles Cardell, his rival and chief critic, and published in the wake of the old man's death. Cardell (1895–1977) had tried, and failed, to buy Gardner's extensive witchcraft museum and would subsequently posit his own 'discovery' of the survival of a parallel underground Pagan tradition, to assert his own leadership of the nascent movement. Although his career would end in bitter controversy and in bankruptcy, after a lost libel case, Cardell's brief, but memorable, account (*Witch*, privately published in

---

[2] R. Buckland, *Ancient & Modern Witchcraft: The Truth about Witchcraft by a Witch High Priest*, (New York: HC, 1970; C. L. Anderson, *A Cauldron of Witches: The Story of Witchcraft*, (New York: Pocket Books, 1973); Lady Sheba (aka J. Wicker Bell), *The Witches Workbook: The Magick Grimoire of Lady Sheba*, (New York: Zebra Books, 1975).

December 1964) set the pattern for many of the subsequent interpretations of Gardner's role in the genesis of modern witchcraft.[3] It castigated him as an 'old showman', the perpetrator of hoaxes, a flagellant, and a 'snob', who after all had been no more than a retired civil servant. Through the testimony of a young woman whom he had paid to infiltrate Gardner's Bricket Wood coven, Gardner emerged as 'a rather querulous invalid' who lacked any great insight into the workings of magic and sought to predate upon vulnerable women. In publishing, in full, the *Book of Shadows* that Gardner had given to his youthful initiate, Cardell was the first to reveal the secret and oath-bound rituals that had accreted, through practice, trial and error, around Gardner's covens. In doing so, he established a text-based approach to what was, essentially, a constantly evolving and experiential religion.

Though his approach was bitterly polemic, and his work revealed him to be both antisemitic and a misogynist, it has proved remarkably durable, as his view of Gardner seeped into the mass market paperbacks of the 1970s, most notably finding expression in Francis King's *Ritual Magic*. King viewed Wicca as an insubstantial offshoot of the Western ceremonial magic, and though he made grudging acknowledgement of Gardner's book, *Witchcraft Today*, and his success in establishing a network of Pagan covens in the wake of its publication, this was more than tempered by the characterisation of Gardner as a Sadomasochist, who built a religion around him in order to satisfy his sexual desires.[4] Again, in keeping with Cardell, he explicitly framed his subject as being a retired member of the 'Malayan customs service', setting an enduring interpretative pattern that sought to locate Gardner within the thought patterns, culture, and prejudices of the British Empire.

If this view slipped, unchallenged, into the academic mainstream, then it was also powerfully re-enforced within the Pagan community by Michael Howard's account of *Modern Wicca*.[5] Howard was the editor and leading light of *The Cauldron*, an influential magazine that acted for more than three decades as a discussion and research journal for the Pagan community. In that capacity, he consistently advanced the idea that a form of 'traditional witchcraft' had survived as an unbroken lineage that was distinct from, and far older than, Gardner's modern creation of Wicca. A charitable view might be that what Howard encountered were fragmentary survivals of the Victorian workings of cunning folk that have been examined in the compellingly original research of

---

[3] Rex Nemorensis (aka C. Cardell), *Witch*, (Charlwood: Dumblecott Magick Productions, 1964).
[4] F. King, *Ritual Magic in England: 1887 to the Present Day*, (London: New English Library, 1970 rpt. 1973), p. 143.
[5] M. Howard, *Modern Wicca: A History from Gerald Gardner to the Present*, (Woodbury: Llewellyn, 2009).

Charles Phythian-Adams and Owen Davies.[6] Whatever the case, there is no evidence to suggest a pattern of survival through hereditary witchcraft at any time before the 1920s.

By this time, it should appear obvious that the beguiling nature of Gardner's original thesis of the endurance of an unbroken, underground, pagan religion was so potent that his critics within the wider esoteric and occult movements were continually appropriating the vision, while jettisoning any contact with the visionary. Rather like the vanishing point in a painting, the search for the origin story of contemporary Pagan witchcraft constantly retreated before its pursuers. In this manner, Howard's thesis required the negation of Gardnerian Wicca in order to validate this idea of a parallel 'witch cult' that otherwise closely resembled it. As a consequence, he characterised Gardner, in the pages of *Modern Wicca* (a book that was heavily reliant for its sources upon the works of amateur historians who had written in *The Cauldron*), as an inveterate publicity seeker, whose prose had to be constantly reworked by his friends and editors in order for it to be made, in any way, publishable.

A further blow, dealt from within the Pagan community, came with the publication of Aidan Kelly's *Crafting the Art of Magic,* in 1991 (later republished and updated as *Inventing Witchcraft* in 2007).[7] This attempted to apply a type of form criticism (more generally associated with the Tubingen School of Biblical exegesis) to the extant working copies of the foundational magical and ritual texts used by Gardner, known collectively as *The Books of Shadows.* Through painstaking research, Kelly revealed the process of constant revision, reworking, and borrowing of comparatively modern or widely available verses, forms, and rites that hallmarked Gardner's distillation of Wicca, between 1949 and 1961. Far from being arcane in origin and the product of the survival of an underground pagan cult, the rituals were shown to have been culled from, amongst other sources, *The Greater Key of Solomon* (a late medieval grimoire that purported to be by the Old Testament king), various cabbalistic works, the writings of Aleister Crowley, and even the poems of Rudyard Kipling. Withering in terms of its revisionism, self-regarding in tone, and dismissive of Gardner's talents and veracity, Kelly's work shone a harsh interpretative light upon *The Book of Shadows* that was intended to be the Gardnerian witch's most secret (literally occult) resource. The difficulty with this approach lies in its

---

[6] C. Phythian-Adams, 'Rural Culture', in G. E. Mingay (ed.), *The Victorian Countryside*, (London, 1981), Vol.II pp. 616–625; O. Davies, *Popular Magic. Cunning Folk in English History*, (London: Hambledon Continuum, 2003).

[7] See, respectively: A. Kelly, *Crafting the Art of Magic, Book I, A History of Modern Witchcraft, 1939–1964*, (St. Paul: Llewellyn, 1991); A. Kelly, *Inventing Witchcraft: A Case Study in the Creation of a New Religion*, (Loughborough: Thoth, 2007).

equation of Wicca's early texts with the practice of the religion, itself, and through a failure to grasp that modern Pagans lie outside the framework of Abrahamic thought, whereby scripture and the revealed word – as opposed to collective and personal experience, and an immersive, and often animistic, relationship with nature – dominate.

Given these developments, Gardner's life and career might have appeared as no more than a strange, and possibly even embarrassing, footnote to the rising trajectory of Wicca had it not been for two, very different, writers who sought to historicise Gardner and modern Paganism. The first was Ronald Hutton, whose *The Triumph of the Moon* first published in 1999 was an academically brave and intellectually brilliant history of the ideas that underpinned the Victorian esoteric revival and fuelled the growth of modern Paganism. It was brave because it could have spelled career suicide at a time when Wicca was viewed in academic circles as being, at best, unworthy of serious engagement and, at worst, foolish and beneath contempt. Its brilliance lay in the ability of the author to move between macro and micro themes, to provide a critical synthesis of a vast esoteric literature, and to deliver an engaging study of both the powerful wellsprings of supportive imagination and the vibrant cultural movements that facilitated the evolution of revived Paganism. It did so in a manner that combined scholarship with sensitivity and respect for the practitioners of magic, and which appealed to both an academic and a popular audience, satisfying both head and heart. An unexpected bestseller, it created an entire mini industry within academia as post-graduate students sought to work, and re-work, the themes and ideas suggested by the book's rich tapestry.

While Gardner appears as very much the foil to his later rival, Alex Sanders (1926–88), Hutton provided a balanced and nuanced account of Gardner's career that was informed by his groundbreaking research in Toronto, among Gardner's surviving papers, and which laid many of the myths woven by both his friends and detractors to rest. Gardner, though an atrocious typist and a phonetic speller, was far from being a dyslexic, and while being fond 'of pretty, nude young women' was neither predatory nor a simple flagellant.[8] Furthermore, while 'he could be devious, and capable of trickery and dissimulation', he was a 'remarkable man', occupying 'the central role' in 'developing and propagating' the revived Paganism that came to be known as Wicca.[9] This verdict, alongside the judicious manner in which Hutton had examined the source material concerning the genesis of Wicca, served to establish Gardner as a highly significant figure in both modern cultural history and the history of ideas.

---

[8] R. Hutton, *The Triumph of the Moon: A History of Modern Pagan Witchcraft*, New Ed., (Oxford: Oxford University Press, 2019), pp. 233, 243.
[9] Hutton, *Triumph of the Moon,* p. 247.

The second figure to re-evaluate Gardner's reputation was Philip Heselton, whose successive biographical studies proved to be true labours of love, and in the case of his two-volume account of *Witchfather. A Life of Gerald Gardner,* published in 2012, did much to strip away persistent myths and accretions through meticulously checking ship rosters, maps, genealogical records, and local directories to locate his subject within the physical and ritual landscapes of South-East Asia and the English counties.[10] *Witchfather* provided a modern, linear as opposed to thematic, biographical study of Gardner which was sympathetic in tone and evidenced many of the claims made in the authorised account of Gardner's life that had been published back in 1960.[11] The popular notion of Gardner as a simple charlatan, 'who made it all up', was effectively challenged and his role as the chief inspiration for – and propagator of – modern witchcraft was championed.

Buoyed by the thorough-going sea change in academia's relationship with witchcraft in its modern form, which now appeared willing to validate Wicca as a religious movement and set of ideas that were worthy of serious investigation and engagement; and rehabilitated in both scholarly and popular accounts, Gardner's reputation was clearly in the ascendant and stands, at present, arguably at a higher point than at any since his death some six decades ago. Yet, just as importantly, the influence exerted by his religious ideas and visions, though often going unacknowledged, has permeated deep into the fabric of modern Western society.

In the 1970s, Michael Benteen (the former Goon) made gentle fun of his claims to have used the operation of magic to favourably influence the outcome of the Battle of Britain on his primetime BBC comedy sketch show, while *Catweazle* (the eponymous hedge witch whose adventures ran on UK children's television for two series, from 1970 to 1971) not only physically resembled Gerald Gardner but also worked recognisably Gardnerian forms of Wicca in his vain attempts to make sense of the modern world. A decade later, Richard 'Kip' Carpenter's re-imagining of *Robin of Sherwood* introduced magic and shamanism to the traditional tales and cast the outlaw band as Pagans living in harmony with the forest and its pre-Christian gods. By 1996, Wicca had reached Hollywood with *The Craft* offering the practice of modern witchcraft as an edgy, yet liberating, path for otherwise alienated young women, while *Practical Magic* – the story of two sisters hailing from a long matriarchal line of witches, who struggle against the bonds wrought by love magic and the prejudice of their smalltown community – achieved major success at the box office two years

---

[10] P. Heselton, *Witchfather: A Life of Gerald Gardner*, 2 vols., (Loughborough: Thoth, 2012).
[11] J. Bracelin, *Gerald Gardner: Witch*, (London: The Octagon Press, 1960).

later. At the turn of the millennium, *Charmed* celebrated female power and sisterhood rooted in the possession of a Gardnerian *Book of Shadows*, while a re-loaded *Sabrina* (loosely based on the teenage witch created for *Archie* comics) brought the themes of gothic horror and the conflict between a vision of diabolism and a benign Gardnarian hodge-podge of herbalism and coven-based magic, to prime time US TV and streaming services from 2018 until its sudden cancellation due to the outbreak of the COVID pandemic in 2020. A tie-in between Marvel Comics and Disney Plus' streaming service resulted in *Agatha Alone*, the story of another teen coven, garnering popular and critical acclaim, and taking the number 1 ratings spot on the Disney Channel when it debuted in September 2024.

If Wicca's coven-based, initiatory, lines number no more than a few thousand members in the United States and Britain; then the clear suggestion is that their cultural significance (and by extension that of Gerald Gardner) far outweighs their numerical strength. Wicca, as Gardner reminded his readers, was never intended as a mass religion. Yet its acceptance by major US corporations as both a largely benign force of personal expression and empowerment, and as a commercial cash cow that consistently delivers when other established franchises have begun to lose their lustre, is suggestive of a marked estrangement from organised religion across Europe and North America and the desire for a direct, pragmatic (and sometimes transactional) form of polytheistic religious expression that accepts the female as divine and the natural world as its most powerful expression.

Indeed, the cultural richness of contemporary Paganism is evidenced and underpinned not just through film and television but through an imaginative and romantic literature that predated Gardner by more than a century (through the likes of Keats, Shelley and Swinburne) to twentieth-century writers as diverse as Kenneth Grahame, Rosemary Sutcliff, Ursula le Guin, Marion Zimmer Bradley, and Deborah Harkness. For poetry and poetic imagination are inextricably bound to Wicca. We are incapable of grasping its essence if we reduce it to exercises in exegesis and form criticism; blinding ourselves to the fact that Gardner was a writer and practitioner steeped in the works of Kipling, Swindburne, Crowley, and Graves, who understood that the act of recovery of a Paganism that had been so thoroughly extirpated between the fourth and fourteenth centuries CE was impossible without forging for it a new, modern – and often modernist – vocabulary. The 'feel' and emotive pull of the verse was far more important to him than its rooting within a specific time frame or cultural sphere. Magpie-like, he plundered an edition of poetry by inter-war Russian émigré writers in order to evoke the recovered memory of a witch burned at the stake and reworked the framing verses of Kipling's *Puck of Pook's*

Hill to provide a Pagan invocation of place, land, and ritual practice.[12] It is, therefore, unsurprising that the most successful and engaging of his successors in the Craft (such as Patricia Crowther and Vivianne Crowley) have acknowledged and appropriated Jungian approaches to mythos and religious archetypes in their writings and practice.

Within this context, Gardner can be seen to have been adept at drawing upon a heterogeneous set of cross-cultural magical practices and to have possessed a remarkable capacity for synthesising imaginative work with popular history. The creative freedom to do so, together with the boldness and lack of restraint that enabled him to fashion Wicca as his own 'rough magic', stemmed from a lifetime of engagement and study that placed him far outset the experiences, and mindset, of the overwhelming majority of Britons who were shaped and took service with the Empire. It is to this background that we now turn.

2 The Magus and the Magic of the Tribe

Gerald Brosseau Gardner was born in Blundellsands, Crosby, on 13 June 1884, the third of four sons of William Gardner (1843–1935), a Liverpool merchant, philanthropist, and Justice of the Peace. The family business, rooted in the supply of African and North American hardwoods for the Mersey dockyards, should have ensured him a life of comfort and privilege, entrance – like his brothers – to the prestigious, nearby, school of Merchant Taylors and access to a choice of professions. However, from the outset, he appeared to be something of a 'cuckoo in the nest' whose childhood was dominated by asthma, an almost complete lack of either parental control or formal education, and by the looming presence of his governess, Georgina McCombie (c.1865–1945). Violent, abusive, and alcohol dependent, McCombie (known as 'Com') took Gardner, as a five-year-old, on the first of an escalating series of foreign travels, officially designed to mitigate his asthma, that saw him journeying from Spain to the Canary Islands, Madeira, and the Gold Coast of North Africa before ranging farther afield into Southeast Asia. Jack Bracelin, Gardner's confidant and official biographer, suggested that 'Com' might well have been the boy's natural mother and though unproven; the contention certainly provides a reason for the remarkable level of parental neglect that characterised his upbringing, split between summers in Blundellsands and winters spent along the equator.[13]

In a highly revealing passage in his official biography, Gardner recalled his governess' change in behaviour towards him from the moment that they first

---

[12] B. Deutsch & A. Yarmolinsky (eds.), *Modern Russian Poetry: An Anthology*, (London: John Lane the Bodley Head Ltd., 1923), p. 79.
[13] L. Bourne, *Dancing with Witches*, (London: Robert Hale, 1998 rpt. 2006), p. 15.

took leave of his parents, and their train rolled out of Liverpool Lime Street station. She refused point-blank to read to him and he immediately discovered the unwelcome shift in the power dynamic governing their relationship, as what he referred to as 'the real Com' asserted herself. On a stop-over in Ghana, the boy – a source of resentment for his governess but a necessary encumbrance if the generous maintenance cheques from the Gardner family were still to arrive on time to fund his upkeep, and her lifestyle – was allowed to roam freely through the streets and bazaars of the port city of Accra. In the evenings, he recalled her holding court to a room full of 'hard-drinking, woman starved planters', watching and listening, 'hating both her and her companions'.[14]

Ignored and probably beaten, Gardner took from his childhood a marked sense of independence, an instinctive curiosity for the world around him, and an ingrained nonconformity that bordered upon rebellion, together with a far less welcome taste for masochism and self-harm. Having taught himself to read, he rapidly progressed from the fairy tales printed in the back pages of *The Strand* magazine, to escapist and esoteric fiction, adventure, and chivalric stories. In particular, he revelled in the works of Florence Marryat and Sir Walter Scott. From Marryat's *There is No Death,* he discovered spiritualism, seances, and a belief in a non-demonic spirit world, animated by female agency; while from Scott's *Ivanhoe,* he took other significant ingredients that informed his own approach to magic, and which would become key to his own later reconfiguring of witchcraft: namely, the archetype of a beautiful and exotic 'witch' in the form of Rebecca, a respect for Judaism, and a fascination with weaponry and the fate of the heretical Knights Templar.[15]

Pushed from pillar to post by his governess' travels, he experienced precious little of organised Christianity but encountered Islam, Hinduism, Buddhism, and the indigenous religions of Southeast Asia without judgement or fixed preconceptions. It seems fair to suggest that, unlike the vast majority of colonialists, he saw no clear distinctions dividing religion from the practice of magic. Furthermore, the absence of exposure to Christian doctrine served to negate the figure of the Devil in both his early and adult thinking. He had dispensed with the idea of 'Hell' on his first reading of Francis Marryat. Magic and witchcraft could, therefore, appear as entirely rational pursuits, aimed at producing practical results that might be effected through contact with spirits or daemons but

---

[14] Bracelin, *Gerald Gardner: Witch,* pp. 15, 17–18.
[15] Bracelin, *Gerald Gardner: Witch,* pp. 19–20; F. Marryat, *There Is No Death*, (New York: National Book Company, No date / 1891); W. Scott, *Ivanhoe: A Romance*, 3 vols., (Edinburgh: Archibald Constable, 1820). It is likely that the young Gardner initially lit upon the abandoned book on spiritualism thinking that the author was Frederick Marryat (the author of 'Boys' Own' style fiction such as *Children of the New* Forest) rather than his daughter, Florence.

which did not stem from either a dualist conception of the world or from the presence of Satan within it. Damnation was neither a threat nor a fear, and death was far from being an ending.

As a consequence, Gardner emerged into young adulthood as an autodidact, occupying a highly ambiguous place within his own family sphere and the colonial society of Southeast Asia. Bright, creative, and good with his hands, he lacked basic academic qualifications and the societal connections that marked out others of his class for success at the heart of the imperial administration. Significantly, his career in colonies was almost entirely based around the liminal areas of imperial influence – in the borderlands between states, the fault lines between tribes and ethnicities, and in the federated and unfederated states of Malaya – rather than in Singapore, the Straits Colony, or garrison outposts. He shunned the 'European clubs', tennis courts, and sailing regattas in favour of trips to the visit the indigenous tribal regions of Malaya and participation in archaeological expeditions to Johore Lama (the ruined former capital of the sultanate subsumed by Malaya), Gaza in Palestine, and Cyprus. Holidays would take him to a China riven by warlords and to French Indo-China (modern-day Vietnam), where he found the temples and palaces of its own imperial city of Hue in ruin, eclipsed by the colonial power.

When we consider these components of his character, alongside the stark fact that the time he spent in the civil service, from 1921 to 1936, accounted for less than half of his working life, the established image of Gerald Gardner as a 'retired civil servant', fully conversant and defined by the mores of class and empire, begins to wither away before our eyes. Though he might choose to adopt the pose of 'Sanders of the River' for his publicity photographs in the 1920s–30s, he was a figure set far apart from those created by C.S. Forrester and G.A. Henty. He belonged, instead, to the shadowlands of empire evoked by Joseph Conrad. He could not turn his back upon the imperial dream because, both culturally and intellectually, he had never been a part of it.

Initially, Gardner's decision to settle and work in the Far East had been determined by Com's marriage to David Elkington, a young tea planter, who had been settled with a large estate in Ceylon (now Sri Lanka) by his wealthy industrial family. If we dismiss the idea of Com being Gardner's natural mother, then his choice as a sixteen-year-old to follow his former governess on her travels and to work for Elkington as a lowly planter, on the 250-acre Ladbroke estate (not to mention Robert Gardner's preparedness to stand security for both his son's wages and board while he did so) appears as nothing short of bizarre.

As it was, Gerald Gardner began his working life as a tea, and then rubber, planter in Ceylon, before moving to North Borneo, in 1910, and Malaya, in 1911, to work on other rubber plantations. Planter culture was rough, physical, entrepreneurial, and emphatically male; and Gardner seems to have excelled in this milieu, where individualism and licence flourished. Yet, beside the practical, there was always the strain of esoteric in the young man's makeup and Gardner joined a freemasons' lodge in Colombo, Sri Lanka, in May 1910, receiving his Master Mason Degree a month later. Though active in the Sphinx Lodge for barely a year and resigning at the time of his move to northern Malaya, he gained from Free Masonry a sense of the workings of a secret society based around initiation. It was a 'craft' which possessed the trappings of ritual magic, and a hierarchy based upon the attainment of successive degrees, at the achievement of which fresh sources of hidden (literally occult) knowledge would be revealed. This hinted at a common route of magical practice, in a period when historians and anthropologists were concerned with seeking commonality across patterns of human behaviour and owned theories of the diffusion of knowledge across cultures from central points. Furthermore, Masonry provided a clear structure for the development, and revelation, of magical practice that suffused not only the Hermetic Order of the Golden Dawn but also Gardner's conception of Wicca.

Attracted by Masonry's hint of the occult and trappings of magic, he seems to have gleaned what he could of the society's rituals before moving on, disillusioned or disinterested by its mundane elements and use as a vehicle for patronage and white, colonial privilege. Indeed, what is often overlooked is that Gardner's imagination, together with his primary experience and practice of magic derived not (as it had from Mathers, Yeats, and Crowley) from an intellectual, text-based, immersion in the Western, Hermetic, tradition, but from the contemporary practice of shamanism and divination among the indigenous religions of the Far East. This was something that he had experienced first-hand, through his contacts with the tribesfolk of Borneo and Malaya, where magic comprised a set of lived – and living – experiences, deployed to practical and, often, worldly ends.

Alongside these developments, as Hugh B. Urban has charted, Gardner's absorption of Hindu Tantrism (from the Western translations and expositions in the work of Sir John Woodroffe), together with his own explorations of Singhalese culture and of the Hindu, Buddhist, and Jain communities of Southern and Eastern Asia, re-enforced his sense of polytheism and the worship of, often, dominant female deities, while introducing him to concepts of guiltless sex and rites performed by couples within a ritual circle.[16] Indeed, Gardner would later stress in his book *The Meaning of Witchcraft* the roles of 'the Great Mother of pre-Aryan India and her horned consort' as religious and cultic

---

[16] H. B. Urban, 'The Goddess and the Great Rite: Hindu Tantra and the Complex Origins of Modern Wicca', in S. Feraro & E. Doyle White (eds.), *Magic and Witchcraft in the Modern West: Celebrating the Twentieth Anniversary of 'The Triumph of the Moon'*, (Eastbourne: Palgrave Macmillan, 2019), pp. 21–39.

archetypes, and of their attendant rites 'among the Tantrics [which] strongly resemble the Western witch covens'.[17] Similarly, he would later take *The Book of Shadows* as the name of his grimoire after reading an article published in *The Occult Observer* in 1949, about a Sanskrit text that sought to judge the fate of an individual by the form and length of their shadow.[18]

However, as with so many areas of Gardner's life, we now run into problems of evidence and interpretation. Our main source for his intellectual and religious development during this period is his official biography, which bears the considerable imprint of Idries Shah's fascination with, and profound understanding of, the magical traditions of the Near and Far East. It could be reasonably argued that its weighting towards Gardner's formative years and encounters with experiential, indigenous, magic might more accurately reflect Shah's priorities and insights rather than his own. Similarly, the passages in Gardner's published account of Malay weaponry that deal specifically with religion and preternatural belief lean heavily upon the, then, standard accounts of magical belief and practice written by European academics. This said, a less reductionist and more generous reading might be to suggest that Gardner's official biography emphasised those very areas that he felt to be important; and that his reliance upon the available specialist literature in forming his own ideas reveals a desire to learn and an engagement with scholarship that has often been hitherto ignored or dismissed. Praxis, whether magical or anthropological, was to be a – and possibly *the* – key component in Gardner's career.

Consequently, over a period of some twenty years, from the 1910s to the 1930s, Gardner witnessed, participated in, and learned from, a series of Shamanistic rituals and beliefs garnered at village level in the Far East among the Dyaks in Borneo; the Senoi (or Saki) in Malaya; and the Krinchi in Sumatra. Here there was an emphasis upon divination, forms of scrying (often by staring into a flame for a protracted period of time) ancestor worship or reincarnation, mediumship, and the making of offerings (often in the form of incense), with music and drumming used to heighten awareness of spirits or of another world. These were mystery religions, often requiring initiation, and worshipping, as in the case of the Dyaks, 'a multitude of small and local deities'.[19] 'Magic', according to Gardner, was thus 'a matter-of-fact affair', whereby:

> Actions and even beliefs were generally related to actuality. Looking at the Saki and other primitive beliefs from this point of view might allow one to hazard the idea that magic *did* work.[20]

---

[17] G. B. Garner, *The Meaning of Witchcraft*, (London: The Acquarian Press, 1959 rpt. 1971), p. 80.
[18] Hutton, *Triumph of the Moon*, pp. 240–241; D. Valiente, *The Rebirth of Witchcraft*, (Marlborough, Wiltshire: Robert Hale, 1989 rpt. 2023), pp. 51–52.
[19] Bracelin, *Gerald Gardner: Witch*, p. 45.   [20] Bracelin, *Gerald Gardner: Witch*, p. 77.

Witnessing the rites of the Tutong tribe in North Borneo, Gardner was impressed by the significance of the *pawang* – or 'witch doctor' – and in attempting to evoke a popular, practical, and efficacious magic for a Western European audience the analogy with the witch's art may have most readily and accurately sprung to mind.[21]

Gardner's contact with indigenous religions and the leisure which afforded him the opportunity for its study were greatly enhanced by his employment in the colonial civil service, initially in the Public Works Department (rebuilding the roads and infrastructure in Malaya) and then as an inspector of rubber plantations, before joining the customs service as an officer policing the opium trade. Gardner fell into the role of a custom's officer, in 1926, at a pivotal moment in the history of the imperial regulation and control of the drugs trade in Southeast Asia.

Opium had defined the economies and colonial regimes of Southeast Asia. Indeed, the taxation, control, and export of the cash crop were core to the maintenance of British imperial power in the region, underwriting the financing of the colonial administration and its attendant military establishment of naval bases and garrisons, without placing additional burdens upon the tax revenue of the Crown. In this manner, the extraction of private profit (from mining, and tea and rubber plantations) could be sustained by what, in theory, was a light and self-sufficient public sphere. However, Great Britain faced heavy censure from the international community, and the United States in particular, at the 1924–25 Geneva Opium Conference for its active participation in the narcotics trade. As a consequence, somewhat shame-facedly, Stanley Baldwin's government promised to introduce the prohibition of both the retail trade and consumption of the drug.[22]

However, such a sudden and drastic reversal of long-standing imperial policy left the colonial administrators in the Crown Colony and the Malay Archipelago struggling to find expedients in order to maintain their own systems of governance and finance that were dependent upon tax revenues garnered from sale of opium. The result was a far more ambiguous commitment to phasing-out the trade that saw the colonial administration assuming control of the colony's opium shops and reducing their number from over 500 to 70. The supply of

---

[21] Bracelin, *Gerald Gardner: Witch*, pp. 45–47; G. B. Gardner, *Keris and Other Malay Weapons*, (Singapore: Progressive, 1936), pp. 43, 55, 57, 59, 61, 128–132.

[22] W. O. Walker III, *Opium and Foreign Policy: The Anglo-American Search for Order in Asia, 1912–1954*, (Chapel Hill: The University of North Carolina Press, 1991), pp. 37–39, 42–45; D. S. Kim, *Empires of Vice: The Rise of Opium Prohibition across Southeast Asia*, (Princeton: Princeton University Press, 2020), pp. 122–123, 148–152.

the drug was regulated and rationed, and, by 1929, some 40,000 (overwhelmingly Chinese) users had been compelled to register with the government.[23]

It was against this background of a profound moral and political crisis that Gardner was employed as a customs officer, to confront the problems of illicit sales and consumption of the drug. Running a 'neat, white launch' through the rivers that crisscrossed the jungles of Johore, Gardner inspected the opium stocks and collected the profits raised from the state opium (or *chandu*) shops, while enforcing the imperial monopoly against interlopers. As with his earlier clashes with rubber smugglers from the Dutch East Indies, he relished the excitement of a chase that often resulted in the ambush and boarding of vessels, with shots fired and prisoners and cargoes taken. It was a life that afforded Gardner the sense of adventure that he had always craved, together with the high degree of licence that suited both his personality and his pocket. Indeed, it seems likely that his large private fortune (that exceeded his generous family inheritance and eclipsed anything he could ever have realised from a modest civil service pension) was founded upon the acceptance of bribes from smugglers and his syphoning of the stocks from the government shops to sell upon the open market.[24] Operating on the margins of an imperial system that was predicated upon, and riven with, corruption; there were few checks upon, or little interest in, his activities.

What is clear is that Gardner, himself, was free from hypocrisy when it came to the operation of the opium trade. He railed against the 'blinkers of a sanctimonious moralising which limited the view of so many the Europeans who had to do with the problem of opium in the Far East' and claimed not to have witnessed the ill-effects of opium upon either individuals or civil society, telling his official biographer that 'I never saw the shambling, broken-down old wrecks of propaganda and fiction, nor anyone even seriously the worse for it'. Thus, his attitude towards the smoking of pure opiates among the Chinese in Malaya stood in stark opposition to his lifelong hatred towards alcohol, and his lasting disdain for the use of cocaine among the European colonisers, and hashish among the Indian workers in both the rubber plantations and *chandu* shops that he supervised.[25] His variable attitude towards narcotics and stimulants was based upon their ability to encourage violence or to stupefy the senses, of which he vigorously disapproved; or to relieve pain, to calm the soul, or to inspire visions, which he saw as being entirely beneficial.

---

[23] D. Mackay, *Eastern Customs: The Customs Service in British Malaya and the Opium Trade*, (London: I.B. Tauris, 2005), pp. 134–136
[24] Bracelin, *Gerald Gardner: Witch*, pp. 67–68, 70–74; Heselton, *Witchfather*, Vol.1, pp. 101–102, 161.
[25] Bracelin, *Gerald Gardner: Witch*, pp. 71–73.

During this period, Gardner's conjoined interests in weaponry, archaeology, and studies of indigenous life and magical beliefs resulted in the publication of his first book, *Keris and Other Malay Weapons*. Its merits have divided scholarly opinion, with, on the one hand, the foremost academic expert on the modern revival of witchcraft regarding it in withering terms, while, on the other, the most recent specialist account of the blade, written in the English language, accorded Gardner's monograph credit as valid and engaging source material.[26] Certainly, at the time of its publication in 1936, it was generously reviewed in the pages of both the colonial press and *The Sunday Times*.[27]

Significantly, Gardner chose to use the Malay rendering of the dagger's name – *Keris* – rather than the most common variant, *Kris*, that dominated Western literature. Such a choice seems to have accorded with his respect for the culture of the indigenous people, and he chose to favourably contrast the heavily ritualised forms of tribal warfare in the Malay Archipelago with the horrors of industrialised European war.[28] As with many of Gardner's writings, there is an air of wistfulness and idealism about the work, in seeking to evoke an a priori culture. Thus, he celebrated the *Keris* as a 'weapon of romance' fallen into disuse through modernity and the colonisers' implementation of the rule of law.

Illustrated with weapons taken from his extensive collection, the book alluded to Gardner's own attempts at experimental archaeology (in attempting to understand and recreate the manufacture of the blades and their hilts) and examined the reputation of the *Kris*, which was frequently fashioned from meteoric iron, as a talismanic or sorcerous weapon. 'Malays', he wrote, 'believe that old things acquire a soul (*semangat*) ... the essence of physical life ... [and] ... It is said that a spirit was attracted to the *Keris* during the making' of the dagger. This spirit was often thought to be female and the blade, once animated, might charm fire, thirst for blood, confer invulnerability, or kill at distance 'merely by being pointed at the victim'.[29] The blade might be lucky or unlucky, depending on its dimensions and in relation to those of its owner's hand; and its power enhanced by the carving of magical signs, names, or verses upon it; growing further with every slain foe.[30] Gardner's later emphasis within Wicca upon the importance of the athame (a black handled knife) as one of the witch's primary tools, and defining possessions certainly owes its conception as a sentient blade to the idea of the

---

[26] Hutton quoted in: Heselton, *Witchfather*, Vol.1, p. 167; E. Frey, *The Kris: Mystic Weapon of the Malay World*, (Oxford: Oxford University Press, 1986), pp. 8–9.
[27] Heselton, *Witchfather*, Vol.1, pp. 143–145.
[28] G. B. Gardner, *Keris and Other Malay Weapons*, (Singapore: Progressive Publishing House, 1936), p. 119.
[29] Gardner, *Keris and Other Malay Weapons*, pp. 10, 11, 14, 16, 55, 57. 61, 128–132.
[30] Gardner, *Keris and Other Malay Weapons*, p. 55.

Keris, imbued with its own spirit and linked to the goddess Shiva as a means to harnessing both creative power and deadly chthonic force.

However, there is another side to Gardner's nature that is expressed within his book and his accent upon the magical power inherent in blades: namely, his fascination with arms and armour. It would be misleading to see the *Keris and Other Malay Weapons* as a work of esotericism. Rather, it is an engaging and workmanlike study of the military culture and expression of the Malays in relation to both indigenous warfare and the devastating impact of gunpowder and Western repeating firearms upon a warrior society that was accustomed to framing conflict within patterns of display, ritual, and individual prowess. His chapters on fortifications, armour, cannon, and small arms run parallel to – and often threaten to eclipse – the central discussion of the significance of the magical blade, and the text is framed within the rationalist and empiricist tone of the European Enlightenment. Gardner sought to understand how – and why – the *Keris* became such a culturally important artefact for Malay warriors, literally disassembling the daggers for the reader's benefit and better understanding and attempting to evoke the mindset of their owners for a sceptical Western audience.[31]

Gardner wrote with a view to forging a name for himself in academia. He had previously published part of his study of the ritual dagger in the journal of *The Malaysian Branch of the Royal Asiatic Society,* in December 1933, and his book and central drive up until the late 1930s appears to have been focused upon the collection, exploration, and exposition of weaponry and armour. During this period, he used his leisure time and financial resources to amass a remarkable collection of around 400 *Keris* daggers and other Malay blades (many of which he would later display in a series of bespoke cabinets in his Manx home), together with indigenous armours, matchlocks, blowpipes, shields, and sleeveless fighting jackets, embroidered with texts from the *Koran* in order to convey immunity from blows and shot. Within this context, it seems fair to suggest that in shaping modern witchcraft, Gardner was keen to formulate a magical practice that satisfied his own interests and passions, giving the ownership and display of weaponry a ritual prominence and significance that was novel and which stemmed, in large measure, from his conception of the indwelling spirits found in the blades of Southeast Asia.

With his book in the presses, Gardner came to a major crossroads in his career. He was owed extensive leave by the colonial government; he discovered that he was eligible for early retirement and a generous pension from the Crown

---

[31] Gardner, *Keris and Other Malay Weapons,* p. 59.

Agents; and he had inherited just short of £3,000 upon the death of his father in August 1935. This sum, together with various trust funds settled upon his wife, Donna, and whatever haul he may have accrued through bribery, corruption, and manipulation of the local opium trade, ensured his financial independence and endowed him with sufficient capital reserves to free him from the constraints of wage labour to pursue his own interests for the rest of his life.

He had wished to remain in Southeast Asia, where he found the climate to be congenial, alleviating his asthma and frequent bronchial infections, and where he had ample scope, in terms of archaeological digs, and access to the collections of the Raffles Museum and Library, and the Batavia Museum, to pursue his military and anthropological studies. However, Donna Gardner was adamant that she wanted to return home to England and Gardner acquiesced, arriving alone in London, in the late spring of 1936, after a stately progress that had seen him take part in the excavation of the fortress gateway of Lachish (in what was then the British mandate of Palestine), visit the 'rose red' city of Petra, the cradle of the ancient Nabatean civilisation, in Transjordan, and journey West through Turkey, the Balkans, a still democratic Austria, and Nazi Germany.

Consequently, by the time of his retirement at the age of fifty-one, he had travelled widely, volunteered as an archaeologist on a number of significant digs, lived in a series of countries where Buddhism, Hinduism, or Islam, as opposed to Christianity, were the dominant faiths, and where living indigenous religions (which we can group together under the umbrella of 'pagan') continued to exist and even flourish (Figure 1). He returned to England, unwillingly,

Figure 1 Gerald Gardner, pictured in 1954, in his new role as 'Director of the Museum of Magic and Witchcraft'. Energetic, sunburned, tattooed, inquisitive, and thoroughly counter-cultural, he stood poised to bring Wicca to the world.

as a relatively young, fit, able and active man, to encounter a largely unfamiliar host culture and gratingly cold autumn and winters and felt compelled to start to piece together a wider purpose for himself, inspired by his forays into the mindsets and ritual practices of the Near and Far East.

3 The Magician: Studies in Praxis

In London, Gardner operated on the fringes of academia, gaining attention through publishing abroad and in translation but found himself largely ignored by British institutions and periodicals. Proud of his personal insights but frustrated by his lack of recognition (and the difficulty in obtaining such basic attributes as a reader's card for the British Library), Gardner now attempted to embroider his scholarly credentials, in September 1937, through the purchase of a bogus doctorate from the improbably named 'Meta Collegiate Extension of the National Electronic Institute', which operated out of a post office box in Nevada, USA.[32] In a hierarchical and class-conscious society, where educational opportunities were overwhelmingly rationed among the elite few, Gardner undoubtedly felt the pressure to compensate, bolstering his social status and claims to intellectual authority. In essence, he sought to buy his way to the top.

If this was not bad enough, then the shadow of plagiarism hangs over Gardner's attempts at securing academic recognition. His published papers were based on a handful of secondary sources, lack references, and are enlivened, largely, by his own practical insights into methods of manufacture, construction, and use of weaponry and early technologies. Their translation into foreign languages accentuated their novelty while limiting close scrutiny. In the case of a paper that he gave, much later at the International Congress on Maritime Folklore and Ethnography held in Naples, in 1954, he was effectively rumbled. Stewart Sanderson, who held the post of Director of the Institute of Dialect and Folk Life Studies at Leeds University, recalled it as 'a scissors and paste job with a sprinkling of folk lore beliefs at the end, based on Basil and Eleanor Megraw "The Development of the Manx Fishing Craft" in *Proceedings of the Isle of Man Natural History and Antiquarian Society* and also an article in *Marriner's Mirror,* April 1941'.[33]

In a bid to escape the winter chills and preserve his health, Gardner took a leisurely Mediterranean cruise, where he visited the museum in Nicosia in

---

[32] Hutton, *Triumph of the Moon,* p. 215; Heselton, *Witchfather,* Vol.1, pp. 166–168.
[33] Stewart Sanderson quoted in: F. Smyth, *Modern Witchcraft: The Fascinating Story of the Rebirth of Paganism and Magic*, (London: Man Myth & Magic / Macdonald Unit 75, 1970), pp. 31–32; E. Megaw, 'Manx Fishing Craft. A Key to Various Types', *The Journal of the Manx Museum*, Vol. V No. 64, (June 1941), pp. 14–16.

order to further his study of Cypriot daggers and began to sketch out a novel that would be self-published, at the close of 1939, as *A Goddess Arrives*. Clunky and complex, the story centres around the theme of reincarnation (as Gardner believed that past life experiences had drawn him back to Cyprus), battles, swordplay, and attempts by an early Cypriot civilisation to repel an invasion by the Egyptians. Gardner seems to have been disinterested in (or simply unaware of) the lure of Classical Paganism, preferring to strip away the mystery of Aphrodite's birth and arrival upon the foamy shoreline at Cythera and reframe her story as a simple confidence trick played by a mortal woman upon the gullible islanders. In Ronald Hutton's words, the novel is very much 'a rationalist and sceptical work' in regard to magic and the cultic centres of Crete and the Aegean.[34]

What he did introduce in the novel is 'a secret witch cult', practised together with many 'witch tricks' by Dayonis, the central female protagonist and fabricator of the myth of Aphrodite.[35] Such a concept stemmed directly from Gardner's reading of the works of Margaret Murray (1863–1963), a trailblazing feminist, archaeologist, and Egyptologist, whose accounts of *The Witch-Cult in Western Europe*, published in 1921, and *The God of the Witches*, published in 1933, made a bold and beguiling case for the survival of witchcraft into medieval and early modern Europe as a direct survival of the fertility- and nature-based indigenous religions of the Palaeolithic Age. If Murray's central thesis has been comprehensively dismantled (initially by Elliot Rose in 1962 and then by a succession of revisionist writers from the 1970s onwards, beginning with Norman Cohn), then, we should recognise that misogyny rendered her as a 'straw woman' in a male-dominated profession and that her work, if poor history enabled great art.

It is worth emphasising that at the point that Gardner encountered her works, Murray stood at the zenith of her career, as a leading expert on the language and religion of ancient Egypt, who had broken through gender's 'glass ceiling' to be appointed as the Assistant Professorship of Egyptology at University College, London, and who, in her retirement, would continue to shape the approaches and focus of the Folk-Lore Society. In the pre-internet age, her authorship of the entry for 'Witchcraft' in the *Encyclopaedia Britannica*, which remained in print from 1929 to 1969, exerted tremendous influence and authority on specialist and non-specialist authors, alike. It was not just Gerald Gardner who fell under

---

[34] Hutton, *Triumph of the Moon*, p. 231.
[35] G. B. Gardner, *A Goddess Arrives*, (London: Arthur H. Stockwell Ltd., undated c.1939), p. 100. It is worth noting that 'Dayonis' was subsequently taken as a magical – or 'witch' – name by an initiate of Gardner's Bricket Wood coven in 1956.

its sway but eminent, mainstream historians of the medieval and early modern periods, such as Steven Runciman and Christopher Hill.

From Gardner's viewpoint, there was first-rate anthropological evidence for a surviving religion practised by the witches – that seemed to bear significant similarities to the indigenous beliefs that he had experienced in the Far East – and which explained, motivated, and endured despite the European persecutions and trials of the sixteenth and seventeenth centuries. This was little short of revelatory and served both to refocus his thoughts upon Western magical traditions and to bring him into the orbit of both Margaret Murray and the Folk-Lore Society. In June 1939, he published an article on 'Witchcraft' in the pages of the *Folk-Lore* journal which sought to examine and provide a provenance for 'a box containing what appear to be witchcraft relics' that had 'come into my possession'. The items included a talisman and staff purporting to have been owned by Matthew Hopkins, the 'witchfinder general', tree bark, hawthorn, and birds' claws, a seal of Solomon worked in lead, a finger bone of a supposed witch, and a 'Witches' Moon-dial' used by them at night, in 'the Seven Hours of Dread'.[36] These were, apparently, pronounced to be genuine by both Margaret Murray and Father John Ward, the proprietor of the Abbey Folk Park and Museum at St. Albans. Yet, they were nothing of the kind and a generous assumption might be that Murray and Ward (who was, then, one of Gardner's friends and close collaborators) simply wished the items to be evidence of English witchcraft and folk belief as it suited the cherished solipsisms that underpinned and empowered their own theories of religion and human development.

Gardner was now pursuing his creative and antiquarian interests – which often blurred in their particulars – while focusing increasingly upon the study of magical systems and their contemporary expressions. Indeed, he would join a wide range of esoteric and initiatory groups over a short period of time, in the 1940s, gaining (just as he had done with the Freemasons) insights and knowledge, while moving quickly and authoritatively through their hierarchical layers of office and degrees. Thus, he joined the priesthood of the Ancient British Church (a Victorian foundation which celebrated bardic culture and a commitment to the restoration of an avowedly Celtic form of Christianity), the council of the Ancient Druid Order (an eighteenth-century revival, which operated primarily as a philanthropic and cultural, as opposed to a religious or Pagan organisation), and attempted to refloat the Ordo Templi Orientis (a secret, magical society, dating from the beginning of the twentieth century, suffused with ideas stemming from Freemasonry, Tantrism, and a romantic attachment to the Knights Templar, which after 1912 was led and reshaped by Aleister Crowley).

---

[36] G. B. Gardner, 'Witchcraft', *Folk-Lore*, Vol. 50, (June 1939), pp. 188–190.

From these eclectic and energetic encounters into mysticism, one can conclude that Gardner possessed tremendous energy; that he was a fast learner with a gift for performing and writing rituals; that he liked 'belonging' to organisations, especially if they were secretive and select; and that he had an attachment to expressions of Celtic, as opposed to English, culture. Indeed, he would fashion an entirely counter-factual backstory for his lineage, rooted in the Scottish Highlands, a witch burning at Newborough in 1640, and an emotional Jacobitism.[37] In more practical terms, both the Ancient British Church and the Ordo Templi Orientis (known as the O.T.O.) were organisations that, by the 1940s, were experiencing terminal decline, haemorrhaging membership, unable to transcend their respective origins in the Victorian religious revival and nineteenth-century European high magic and esotericism. Out-of-step with modernity, their faltering structures appealed to Gardner's fondness for lost causes and may have appeared ripe, to his acquisitive eyes, for a takeover and comprehensive reframing.

However, all these initiatives rapidly paled into insignificance when compared to his engagement with witchcraft. Gardner had moved from London, in 1938, settling in Highcliffe, on the fringes of the New Forest, to be close to Com Elkington (as she was then known), who had retired to Bournemouth. Here, we are confronted by the strong (if fraught and abusive) bonds that tied Gardner, even in middle age, to his former governess. True to form, once in Highcliffe, Gardner joined a range of local groups (ranging from everything from local history to naturism, and from civil defence to the Conservative Party). The most significant of these was the newly built Rosicrucian Theatre in neighbouring Christchurch, which staged amateur theatricals loosely based around esoteric themes, and provided a fulcrum for a diverse group of individuals interested in theosophy and with a background in Co-Masonry.

Bournemouth was a flourishing resort and, in the early twentieth century, a congenial home for bohemians such as the Tolstoy colony (who established a community inspired by the writer's egalitarian and mystical teachings) and the Besant family. Annie Besant (1847–1933) had won fame as a pioneer feminist and socialist, who had provided the effective stimulus for modern trade unionism through her campaigning alongside the London match-women in 1888. Yet, if her political impulses found their expression in Marxism, as the theoretic and practical system most suited to the liberation of women, then her religious expression – similarly attuned and reflected through her feminism – found its inspiration in theosophy, as a set of mystical and moral beliefs shaped by, and open to, women alongside men. After travelling to India, she founded Co-Masonry in 1902, as an initiatory body that removed the bars placed upon women from receiving

---

[37] Bracelin, *Gerald Gardner: Witch*, p. 165.

membership, and by extension learning the secrets, of the Freemasons. Her daughter, Mabel Besant-Scott (1870–1952), took on her mantle after her death and, despite secessions and schisms within Co-Masonry, held together a small, but vibrant, band of followers in the Bournemouth area, under the banner of the Rosicrucian Order of Crotona Fellowship.

It was this group which Gardner encountered and befriended at Christchurch, and it is reasonable to suggest that they were firmly counter-cultural in terms of their dress, free thought, conceptions of gender equality, sex, and attitudes to Christianity and expressions of organised religion. Influenced by themes drawn from Hinduism and Buddhism, as well as the Rosicrucian ideal of mystical personal and political unions capable of improving and enlightening the human condition, Gardner would have felt an immediate pull towards people who shared his interests in reincarnation, divination, a nature that was sentient and a world that was animated by spirits.

Much later, Gardner recalled that he:

> noticed a group of people apart from the rest [at the Rosicrucian Theatre]. They seemed rather brow-beaten by the others, kept themselves to themselves. They were the most interesting element, however. Unlike many of the others, they had to earn their livings, were cheerful and optimistic and had a real interest in the occult. They had carefully read many books on the subject: Unlike the general mass, who were supposed to have read all but seemed to know nothing.[38]

This passage is revealing in that it displays those qualities (of creativity, productivity, and optimism about the world and individual capacities) that Gardner would seek to place at the very heart of Wicca. Unsurprisingly, this little sub-group within the Crotona Fellowship conformed to (or perhaps distilled) his ideals and reached-out to Gardner, suggesting that they had known him over the course of a previous lifetime, and (as Gardner claimed) both revealed their true nature as members of a surviving witch-cult and accepted him for initiation into their New Forest coven, in September 1939.

This then, is the genesis – or founding story – of Wicca. It has been examined, explored, and embroidered at great length over recent years. It may be no more than myth. Yet, for our purposes, it is worth highlighting two features within it. The first is Gardner's own sense of self-realisation, wonder, and liberation at what he felt that he had encountered:

> I then knew that that which I had thought burnt out hundreds of years ago still survived ... How wonderful; to think that these things still survive.[39]

---

[38] Bracelin, *Gerald Gardner: Witch*, pp. 164–165.
[39] Bracelin, *Gerald Gardner: Witch*, pp. 165–166.

The second is that whatever may, or may not, have been practiced between Gardner and this small circle of friends, between 1939 and 1944, they were not operating in an intellectual and cultural vacuum. Individuals as different as Rupert Brooke, Robert Graves, Dion Fortune, Aleister Crowley, and Alexander Keiller had already attempted to practice a form of revived Paganism based around the worship of nature, elements of ritual magic, and a pantheism that often stressed the immanence of a horned god. Moreover, in the wake of the publication of Margaret Murray's *Witch-Cult in Western Europe,* a rich seam of imaginative literature opened up that either postulated or wished-for the continuing existence of an underground tradition of coven-based witchcraft. This stretched from Theda Kenyon's *Witches Still Live,* that posited 'modern witchcraft' as a thriving 'nature cult', to the superlative modernist feminist fiction of Sylvia Townsend Warner and Mary Webb, and the blurring of the edges between imaginative literature and historical investigation in the works of Hugh Ross Williamson from which Gardner took the conception of witchcraft as being 'the Craft of the Wise'.[40]

Life was mirroring art, and Murray's work provided the interpretative framework and the imaginative stimulus for Gardner to begin to use 'witchcraft' as an umbrella term to describe a highly heterogeneous set of beliefs, practices, and magical workings that, as Ronald Hutton has demonstrated in *The Triumph of the Moon* had been rekindled by the new freedoms conveyed by the European Enlightenment and reforged by nineteenth-century Romanticism. Moreover, through the 1940s, he came increasingly to use the term 'witch' to define his own person, practice, and relationship with magical power. This was an entirely new development, in breaking with the figure of the magus, warlock, or necromantic magician, in order to subsume masculine practice within an identity that, hitherto, had popularly been held as feminine.

In another of Wicca's founding myths, Gardner celebrated the holding of rituals in the New Forest to prevent Hitler's projected invasion of Britain, in the summer of 1940, as 'Operation Cone of Power': a decisive event, enacted by witches (probably as a form of sex magic and thought projection), drawn from all over the country. During the post-war period, he delighted in retelling the story in private to friends and confidants, such as Jack Bracelin and Patricia Crowther, and in public through a stream of newspaper articles, interviews, and in his two books on witchcraft. He was immensely proud of the act, framing it

---

[40] T. Kenyon, *Witches Still Live: A Study of the Black Art To-Day,* (London: Rider, 1931); S. Townsend Warner, *Lolly Willows, or the Loving Huntsman,* (Milton Keynes: Penguin Classics, 1926 rpt. 2020); M. Webb, *Precious Bane,* (London: Jonathan Cape, 1924 rpt. 1941); H. Ross Williamson, *The Silver Bowl,* (London: The New English Library, 1948 rpt. 1961), pp. 50–51.

Oates, C., & Wood, J., *A Coven of Scholars: Margaret Murray and her Working Methods*, (London: The Folklore Society, 1998).

Pearson, J., Roberts, R. H., & Samuel, G., (eds.), *Nature Religion Today: Paganism in the Modern World*, (Edinburgh: Edinburgh University Press, 1998).

Pearson, J., *Wicca and the Christian Heritage: Ritual, Sex, and Magic*, (London: Routledge, 2007).

'Rex Nemorensis' (aka Cardell, C.), *Witch*, 2nd ed., (Charlwood: Dumblecott Magick Productions, 1964).

Rose, E., *A Razor for a Goat: A Discussion of Certain Problems in the History of Witchcraft and Diabolism*, intro. R. Kieckheffer, (Toronto: University of Toronto Press, 1962 rpt. 2003).

Sheppard, K. L., *The Life of Margaret Alice Murray: A Woman's Work in Archaeology*, (Lanham, Maryland: Lexington Books, 2013).

Starhawk (pseud. Simos, M.), *The Spiral Dance: A Rebirth of the Ancient Religion of the Great Goddess*, 10th anniversary ed., (New York: HarperSanFrancisco, 1979 rpt. 1989).

Teare, T. D. G., *Folk-Doctor's Island*, (Douglas: Times Press, 1963 rpt. 1964).

Urban, H. B., 'The Goddess and the Great Rite: Hindu Tantra and the Complex Origins of Modern Wicca', in Feraro, S., & White, E. D., (eds.), *Magic and Witchcraft in the Modern West: Celebrating the Twentieth Anniversary of the Triumph of the Moon*, (Eastbourne: Palgrave Macmillan, 2019), pp. 21–43.

Valiente, D., 'Gerald Brosseau Gardner', in Valiente, D., (ed.), *An ABC of Witchcraft, Past and Present*, (London: Robert Hale, 1973 rpt. 1994), pp.152–158.

Valiente, D., *The Rebirth of Witchcraft*, (London: Robert Hale, 1989 rpt. 2007).

White, R., *The Witches House: Cecil Williamson and his museums*, (no place: Antenna, 2025).

within a wider narrative of service to the nation by organised covens of witches, who appeared whenever England was threatened to save the country from invasion by both the Armada, in 1588, and Napoleon, in 1803–05.

It is not unreasonable to think that at a time of the Blitz, existential fears would manifest themselves through spiritual, invocatory practices such as the performance of rites, the saying of prayers, and the gift of offerings. In Church services across the land, higher aid was sought on a daily basis for the nation's preservation and the safe return of loved ones from the war. Amidst the horror of such a crisis, a similar catharsis may have been experienced by those practicing magic and esoteric religion. We know that Dion Fortune (1890–1946), a founder of the Fraternity of the Inner Light and promoter of Glastonbury Tor as a place of mystical and ecstatic energy, organised weekly meditations in order to project the idea of peace, encouraged the members of her magical order to repeat a protective mantra during air raids, and envisaged her own angelic host rising-up to protect the Dover coast from landings.[41]

Within this context, it is plausible that Gardner did *something* (enacting a series of protective rites with a small group of friends in the New Forest) with the intention of preventing the Wehrmacht from crossing the Channel. However, to frame this rite as part of a pre-existing form of Wicca is unsupported by anything resembling evidence; while to suggest that it was decisive in the defeat of the Luftwaffe in the Battle of Britain is risible and more than a little tasteless. What is probable is that, post-war, Gardner was keen to accentuate the importance of this symbolic act in order to demonstrate the selflessness and patriotism of those whom he was coming to style as witches. The witch, so long reviled as an enemy within the host society, was now being portrayed as its friend and saviour.

Furthermore, this was one of the few occasions when Gardner chose to intrude upon the realm of politics. He did so to distance his own form of revived witchcraft from other currents within the occult movement that had explicitly linked themselves, and their fortunes, to the rise of Nazism and the promotion of theories of Aryan racial and spiritual superiority. If we look at those who stood at the centre of occultism during the inter-war years, and some of those practitioners whom Gardner mixed with and promoted, during the post-war period, then one sees a grim and sorry tale of political reaction, racial hatred, antisemitism, and a glorification of militarism. General Fuller was a leading member of the British Union of Fascists (BUF) and was interned during wartime; Dennis Wheatley was an imperialist who embraced fascism during the 1930s and used his post-war

---

[41] D. Fortune, *The Magical Battle of Britain* (Bradford on Avon: Golden Gates Press, 1993), pp. 18, 29–30, 36.

fiction to link the political Left to Satanism; while Alexander Cannon was a Nazi sympathiser, and possible spy, whose wartime movements were shadowed by the state. Closer to home, Barbara Vickers (one of Gardner's first initiates into Wicca) had been a long-standing member of the BUF, while Doreen Valiente, who is more usually remembered for her social liberalism and connections, through her first husband, to Republican Spain, would join both the National Front and the Northern League (another Neo-Nazi outfit with para-military pretensions), in the early 1970s, in attempt to link to Nordic Heathenism with the forging 'of political wing of the Old Religion'.[42]

It was only during the 1950s and early 1960s that Gardner's friendship group began to clearly reflect markedly different values, with the introduction of Arnold Crowther, an anti-racist who despised Colonialism; Patricia Crowther, a lifelong vegetarian, who had a radical campaigning commitment to animal rights; Jack Bracelin, who embraced the radical Left and counter-culture of the 1960s; and Angus Macleod, a Socialist, environmentalist, and member of CND. Thus, Gardner's Conservatism and libertarianism, which revealed itself in its rejection of the establishment of the NHS and fear of uniformity through state planning and Socialism, might appear relatively mild given the disproportionate influence of the Hard Right over the occult during the 1930s–40s.

Gardner's hatred of Nazism was long-standing and genuine. Its expressions of militarism, brutality, and total disregard for anything, or anyone, that stood outside its own world view, sickened him. He could be found arming his fellow Air Raid Wardens and the local Home Guard with weapons culled from his own collection and even attempted to press his nineteenth-century Malay cannon into service against the would-be invaders, scouring the county for gunpowder and shot, and delighting in the thought of the mayhem he could cause with it. He was at his plucky best with a letter, published in *The Daily Telegraph* on 13 August 1940, in which he advocated popular resistance against an invading army and in the pages of the *Christchurch Times*, later in the month, when he reflected that 'As to annoying the Nazis, Dr. Gardner says he does not like annoying anybody, but in this case it affords him very much pleasure'.[43] In adding a patriotic component to the foundation myth of Wicca, he was thus both striking against Nazism and creating clear blue water between his vision of a positive, tolerant, and essentially humanistic form of magical practice, and the drive for political, personal, and sexual domination sought, and popularised, by Crowley, Fuller, and Wheatley.

---

[42] P. Heselton, *Doreen Valiente: Witch*, (Milton Keynes: Doreen Valiente Foundation in Association with the Centre for Pagan Studies, 2016), p. 162.
[43] Heselton, *Witchfather,* Vol. 1, pp. 231–232.

In terms of a simple timeline, we are left with these two pivotal accounts of his discovery of the lost 'witch-cult' and participation in a New Forest rite, in 1939 and 1940 respectively. We are then confronted by a long gap before the first surviving edition of his grimoire, or *Book of Shadows*, was compiled in the late 1940s and he appeared at the opening of Cecil Williamson's museum on the Isle of Man, in 1951, as 'the resident witch'. Given this lack of evidence and what we know of his other activities in the 1940s (his involvement with the Ancient British Church, the Ancient Order of Druids, and the O.T.O.), it seems reasonable to suggest that his contact with a splinter group of the Crotona Fellowship had proved his lasting inspiration but that whatever group practice they had pursued had fizzled out within a couple of years. This left him searching for a magical system capable of sustaining and developing his vision, and with the growing feeling that witchcraft, as opposed to Druidry or the High Magic of the Order of the Golden Dawn, most accurately evoked and corresponded to it. If Wicca had been coherent in its form and practices in 1939–40, then he would never have needed to have embarked on a quest for sources, insights, and authority over the course of the rest of the decade.

His search led him to the door of Aleister Crowley (1875–1947). He was introduced through his friend, the stage magician and puppeteer, Arnold Crowther (1909–74), on 1 May 1947 and met with Crowley (according to the evidence of Crowley's diary) on three subsequent occasions, the last being on 27 May 1947. They also maintained a brief correspondence, mainly concerning the not inconsiderable financial payments that Gardner had made to gain initiation into the higher degrees of the O.T.O. The context of their brief relationship was, therefore, amicable but essentially transactional. Gardner wished to progress swiftly through the grades of Crowley's last magical order and was awarded (or purchased) a charter that conveyed upon him the right to lead a revived branch of the O.T.O. in England. At this point, Crowley had retired to a small flat in a villa in Hastings. He was still writing, though terminally ill, in straightened financial circumstances, and anxious about the survival of his legacy and the future of his order, which if thriving in North America and the Allied zone of Western Germany was moribund in Britain. Gardner was, thus, one of several aspiring magicians whom he promoted through the initiatory grades at breakneck speed and sought to trust in the hopes that they might revitalise Thelema.[44]

Alongside his charter and Crowley's devolved authority, Gardner gained his initiatory name – 'Scrire' (from the Latin meaning 'to know') – which became

---

[44] R. Kaczynski, *Perdurabo: The Life of Aleister Crowley*, revised & expanded ed., (Berkeley: North Atlantic Books, 2010), pp. 542–544, 553.

both his pen name in the 1940s and the 'witch name' that he would use during rituals for the rest of his life; the injunction to 'Perfect and perfect trust' which he threaded through Wicca; and an acquaintance with high magic and Crowley's poetry from which he borrowed liberally, although not always accurately.[45] Among Crowley's wider circle of followers, he borrowed the incantation 'Eko! Eko! Azarak!' from an article written by Fuller in 1921 (which he would later use in his novel, *High Magic's Aid,* as well as in his own ritual circles), and was lent a number of books by Gerald Yorke, including *The Key of Solomon,* that provided the cornerstones of the rites revealed in *High Magic's Aid* and incorporated within the earliest versions of Gardner's *Book of Shadows.*[46]

Yet, Gardner's foray into ceremonial magic proved something of a dead end. He had planned a summer camp to re-energise the English O.T.O. and crossed the Atlantic, in late 1947, meeting with Karl Germer, the representative of the North American chapter, in early 1948.[47] The encounter was ostensibly a success as Germer confirmed him as the head of the order in Europe and gifted him the status through office which he had always craved. However, after using his new title to attempt to purchase papers and artefacts from Crowley's estate, Gardner's interest rapidly waned, and the proposed camp never materialised. Having talked and bought his way to a position of authority, as a putative heir to Crowley, his sudden abandonment of the O.T.O. appears strange and even self-defeating. Poor health may have played a part, as Gardner complained of asthma attacks, the debilitating cold, and failing energy levels, throughout this period. However, it is more likely that a combination of a lack of application in the study and practice of O.T.O. rituals and the growing realisation that Crowley's form of high magic did not fit with his own vision of a feminised nature religion led to his disenchantment and detachment. Put simply, in Philip Heselton's words, Gardner found himself 'out of his depth' and retreated to the English countryside.[48]

Gardner had already attempted to salvage objects and buildings from the Abbey Folk Park in New Barnet. This had been founded by J.S.M. Ward in 1934 as the first open air museum in the United Kingdom, reconstructing historic buildings threatened with demolition and displaying everyday objects with a view to encouraging an interest in, and the study of, social history. Gardner was fascinated by the project and by the survival of what Ward had described, in

---

[45] Kaczynski, *Perdurabo: The Life of Aleister Crowley,* p. 543. See also: C. Harper quoted in Heselton, *Witchfather,* Vol. 2, pp. 350, 354–355.
[46] Kaczynski, *Perdurabo,* p. 614 endnote 78; Hutton, *Triumph of the Moon,* pp. 229, 234–235, 237; A. J. Trythall, *'Boney' Fuller: The Intellectual General, 1878–1966* (London: Cassell,1977), pp. 20–21, 24–26, 107, 221.
[47] Hutton, *Triumph of the Moon,* p. 230.   [48] Heselton, *Witchfather,* Vol.2, p. 369.

1936, as a sixteenth-century, half-timbered, 'Witch's Cottage'.[49] With the Folk Park losing money after its wartime closure and Ward's own mystical order, the Confraternity of the Kingdom of Christ, looking for a new home: Gardner stepped, offering to exchange the cottage for land he had bought in Cyprus in the 1930s. With the deal concluded, Gardner sought to establish his own version of the Folk Park, relocating the cottage (which was probably a composite of several different buildings, including an old apple store) to the grounds of the Bricket Wood naturist camp, in which he had shares and would come to own.

Gardner now possessed an attractive and atmospheric base that seemed to link him to the practices of historical witchcraft, and began fashion his own vision around it. Drawing inspiration from James Frazer's *Golden Bough* (originally published in 1890), and crystallising around the work of Margaret Murray in the inter-war period, giving credence to the idea of the survival of a fertility cult of great antiquity, Gardner found its wistful expression across a range of literary sources and came to hope that it might be reconnected with, or called back to into being. Charles Leland, a North American folklorist, had claimed to have found fragmentary survivals as early as 1899, that he published as *Aradia, or the Gospel of the Witches,* based upon oral testimony gathered from the Romagna in Northern Italy; while, in 1919, the classicist, Dudley Wright ventured (in a book on the *Eleusinian Mysteries* that Gardner owned and quoted from) that 'It is certain that many rites of the pagan religion were performed under the dissembled names of convivial meetings, long after the publication of the Emperor's edicts ... and were never totally suppressed'.[50] Robert Graves' *The White Goddess* had evoked the figure of a universal, mother goddess and ascribed the kernel of all creative and poetic impulses to an engagement with the female, pagan, and matriarchal muse. He would go on to advocate the creation of a modern Paganism, uniting magical currents drawn from both the East and West, but with Idries Shah, as opposed to Gerald Gardner, as its progenitor. In a similar fashion, Walter W. Gill, another folklorist directly inspired by Frazer's *Golden Bough,* wrote in 1933 that witchcraft:

> ever since its emergence from prehistoric darkness, has been almost exclusively a women's religion, and hence would appear to stand a chance of returning to fashion, with a little alteration and retrimming.[51]

---

[49] A. R. Baker, 'The Scholar the Builders Rejected – The Life & Work of J.S.M. Ward', *Ars Quatuor Coronatorum: Being the Proceedings of Quator Coronati Lodge No. 2076*, Vol. 116, (October 2004), p. 170.

[50] D. Wright, *The Eleusinian Mysteries and Rites*, (London: The Theosophical Publishing House, 1919), pp. 46–47. See also: G. B. Gardner, *The Meaning of Witchcraft* (London: The Aquarian Press, 1959 rpt. 1971), pp. 86–87.

[51] W. W. Gill, *A Second Manx Scrapbook*, (London: Arrowsmith, no date, c.1932), pp. 167–168.

Though Gardner was probably not aware of Gill's work until the early 1950s, this sense of 'a little alteration' and 'retrimming' of a form of Pagan witchcraft was precisely what Gardner had embarked upon in the 1940s and which would dominate the remainder of his life.

4 The Sun and the Moon: Fashioning Wicca and Writing Witchcraft

Gardner's initial engagement with witchcraft made manifest through the publication, in 1949, of his historical novel *High Magic's Aid* was shaped by the legal constrictions placed upon magical practitioners by the provisions of the 1736 Witchcraft Act. Published by Michael Houghton, the owner of London's *Atlantis* bookshop, with Gardner providing a generous subsidy to cover the printing costs, the book was intended to make the author's name within the occult community and to impart that which an underground religion 'believed and attempted to achieve'.[52] As fiction, it is ponderous, poorly plotted, and derivative, taking its inspiration from Sir Walter Scott's *Ivanhoe* and some of its phrasing from John Buchan's short story, *The Grove of Ashtaroth*. As history, it is a non-starter, revealing Gardner to have very little grasp of the culture, society, and politics of thirteenth-century England. However, in terms of its fashioning of ideas, themes, and moods that would later find their expression in Wicca, it is fascinating.

The quest at the heart of the story involves the search for, and forging of, the witch's magical tools (namely, a sword blade; a black handled dagger, or athame, and a white handled knife), and the initiation of the leading male characters into a flourishing 'Witch Cult' by Morven, a young, female, witch. Fuller's invocatory chant is included as part of Medieval ritual, together with Crowley's injunction to 'Perfect Love and perfect Trust', while the casting of a magical, protective circle, the initiatory rites of the first and second (if not the third) degrees of the mystery religion, and a guide to the manufacture of 'the Talismans, Sigils and Pentacles' would feed seamlessly into what would subsequently become known as Wicca. If Gardner's accomplished illustrations on the endpapers of the book derived primarily from the images of the layout of 'the Great Circle', together with ritual blades, sprinklers, sigils, and astrological talismans, contained within the edition of MacGregor Mathers' 1888 edition of *The Key of Solomon,* then at least he was open about this one particular intellectual debt.[53]

---

[52] G. B. Gardner, *High Magic's Aid*, (Milton Keynes: Aurina Books, c.1939–40 rpt. 2010), p. 8.
[53] Gardner, *High Magic's Aid,* pp. 8, 46, 123–125, 131, 207–208, 222, 240–241, 244.

More interesting are the insights into Gardner's own conception of witchcraft. It was female led and inspired; it was avowedly Pagan (as those tried for the crime in Western Europe in the sixteenth and seventeenth centuries were not); it placed an accent upon ritual nudity in order to increase the efficacy of spells; believed in reincarnation; and employed techniques of invocation, scrying, altered consciousness, and divination, together with music, in order to achieve its effects. Despite the title of his novel, Gardner was not operating a system of 'high magic' at all. Instead, the beliefs and practices that he evoked spoke of a far rougher magic, rooted at village level, among cunning folk, the poor, and the oppressed. The magus (or male magician), familiar to his audience through the works of Crowley and Wheatley was removed from the scene and, significantly, the devil (or any sense of demonic magic) were completely absent. It is here, in rejecting (or at this point simply ignoring) demonology, that Gardner was breaking entirely new ground in the history of witchcraft. Indeed, he was thoroughly subverting its form and substance.

Witches became the guarantors and not the despoilers of the crop; their tinctures cured rather than killed; and they became the essence as opposed to the enemy of both the nation state and the planet's ecology. Their polytheistic gods (male, female, and possibly even neuter) were *the* 'old gods, who are love, and goodness, kindness and pleasure'.[54] 'They are', Gardner tells us:

> good, at least, to us, but are not all-powerful, and so they *need* our aid. They desire fertility, for man, beasts, and crops, but they need our help to bring it about.[55]

Herein, lay the over-riding conception of Wicca. Positivist and humanist, it stood in creative tension with the natural world, and in opposition to organised religion in Western Europe, with its emphasis upon doctrine, original sin, and the subjugation of the individual before a single, almighty force. In an age of conformity, austerity, and (by the mid-1950s) of overt reaction, this represented a heady, counter-cultural cocktail.

Additionally, Gardner provided witchcraft with a doctrine of resistance. In the introduction to his novel, he proclaimed that 'At least about nine millions of [the witches] suffered a cruel death, mainly by being burned alive, because of this belief'.[56] This figure came from his reading of Matilda Joslyn Gage's seminal work on feminism and provided, particularly for Second Wave feminists and the development of Wicca through environmental and political activism

---

[54] Gardner, *High Magic's Aid*, p. 58. [55] Gardner, *High Magic's Aid*, p. 71.
[56] Gardner, *High Magic's Aid*, p. 7.

in the 1970s–80s, a casus belli in the struggle against authoritarian, patriarchal, and theocratic violence.

High Magic's Aid stands as Wicca's founding document and Gardner, despite attempting to occlude its roots in his own distinctive, personal vision, certainly saw it in this way. It also marked a sea change in Gardner's writing, with the abandonment of any attempt to rationalise witchcraft: magic really did, from now on, have the power to transform human conditions; and immanent gods existed rather than being the products of credulity. The book would be given to those interested in pursuing initiation (such as Patricia Crowther and Lois Bourne) in order to reveal core practices and essential spirit that animated Pagan witchcraft.

The decisive societal break with the past came in 1951 with the repeal of the Witchcraft Statute of 1736. During the first half of the twentieth century this legislation had been used as a catch-all measure for the prosecution of Romany fortune tellers, spiritualists, astrologers, and cunning folk. It also threatened to spark a moral panic given the popular association of witchcraft, through the works of Dennis Wheatley with demonology, moral degeneracy, cruelty, and blood sacrifice. Consequently, an extended campaign led by the National Spiritualists Association was launched over the course of the late 1940s, and Gardner proved himself to be an indefatigable and adept lobbyist, deluging MPs on all sides of the House of Commons with letters urging a change in legislation. While he was not at the forefront of the national campaign and public debate, he certainly felt that the passage of the Fraudulent Mediums Act, in early 1951, was a personal triumph and vindication, fully appreciating its significance and the new opportunities presented.

Herein lay the essential tension between Wicca and the host society in which it operates. The freedom to self-define and operate as a magical practitioner is predicated upon the rationalist basis of a legal system and a dominant culture that deny the efficacy of those self-same forces. Revived witchcraft may often sneer at the values of the European Enlightenment, but it requires them and owes them a central debt, in granting its religious freedom. As Gardner fully understood, everything flowed and was made possible by the legislative changes enacted in 1951.

Yet, he was not the first to take advantage of the new civil liberties to go into print upon the subject. Instead, it was Pennethorne Hughes, a former public school teacher and Human Resources officer at the BBC, who published an account of *Witchcraft* to coincide with the easing of legal restrictions. Heavily influenced by the works of Margaret Murray, as well as by those of Montague Summers (a self-styled cleric and opponent of what he saw as Satanic practices), Hughes provided a popular account of ancient and early modern witchcraft that accepted, and promoted, the idea of a covert, initiatory, 'witch cult' that held sabbats and practised a mixture of 'deliberate diabolism' and 'cruel nonsense'. Though his scorn was mainly directed at Aleister Crowley, he did consider whether there might be a revival of a modern form of witchcraft. His answer was unambiguous:

> For witchcraft, as a cult-belief in Europe, is dead. As a degenerate form of a primitive fertility belief, incorporating the earliest instructive wisdom, the practice is over. Conjurers, wisewomen, palmists and perverts, may be called witches, but it is using an old stick to beat a dead dog.[57]

Enraged, Gardner wrote a counterblast that would be published, in 1954, as *Witchcraft Today*. This was, and remains, Wicca's seminal account and was conceived as the story of witchcraft practice written from the inside. Indeed, its title page proudly proclaimed Gardner to be a 'Member of one of the ancient covens of the Witch Cult which still survive in England' (the 'cult', or 'cultus' in this context being no more than an expression of the witches' manner of worship). His foreword to the book explicitly laid challenge to Hughes' work. 'I have been told by witches in England', he began, that he should:

> Write and tell people we are not perverts. We are decent people, we only want to be left alone, but there are certain secrets that you mustn't give away.[58]

This together with his title as 'Director of the Museum of Magic and Witchcraft, Castletown, Isle of Man', and an introduction offered by Margaret Murray (that agreed with his central thesis that 'much of ... so-called "witchcraft" is descended from ancient rituals') appeared to establish Gardner as an authority on the subject, whose personal praxis and role as an anthropologist, afforded him unique insights.[59] At its kernel, Gardner acknowledged that witchcraft remained a mystery religion and, importantly, defined himself as being just one of a wider collective, who was not a leader or privy to an understanding of all its workings, rationales, and secrets. Such an approach was important for two reasons. Firstly, because it established Gardner's own relationship to what would become known as Wicca. As with the gods he worshipped, he did not pretend infallibility, wish to be celebrated for his own sake, or seek the attainment and wielding of power.[60] This set him apart from those leaders of new religions

---

[57] P. Hughes, *Witchcraft*, (London: Longman, 1952 rpt. 1972), p. 204.
[58] G. B. Gardner, *Witchcraft Today*, (London: Rider and Company, 1954 rpt. 1956), p. 13.
[59] Gardner, *Witchcraft Today*, pp. 13, 16. In fact, Murray is equivocal in her endorsement, using her introduction to revisit her own ideas and to do no more than to report that 'Dr. Gardner states that he has found in various parts of England groups of people who still practise the same rites as the so-called "witches" of the Middle Ages, and that the rites are a true survival' (op.cit. p.15). This is a precis of the book's argument, not an acceptance of its veracity.
[60] Gardner, *Witchcraft Today*, p. 138.

whose cults of the personality negate the role of all other practitioners and render them supplicant. Secondly, it placed a critical distance between Gardner and the people and practices that he was attempting to describe. He could only reveal what he was allowed to by the other members of the underground cult and was engaged in taking the reader on a journey of personal exploration.

Such an approach may have been no more than an exercise in 'smoke and mirrors'. Whatever Gardner did, or did not, experience in the New Forest, it was certainly not contact with an unvarnished, and unbroken, seam of Palaeolithic religion. Moreover, evidence for his contacts with practising and self-defining witches, let alone recognisable covens, is fraught with interpretative difficulty. The first witch to have practised alongside him seems to have been Edith Woodford-Grimes (1887–1975), an elocution teacher, whom he had encountered through the Rosicrucian Fellowship in Christchurch, and who by the mid-1940s had become his mistress and creative partner in the exploration and working of a form of nature based, practical magic that we can think of as being recognisably Pagan.[61] Theirs was a relationship of equals; and she acted as High Priestess to Gardner. However, the 'Southern Coven' of which Gardner wrote, and frequently alluded, comprised no more than themselves, alongside a shifting presence of a handful of other individuals, from approximately 1946 to the end of 1952. Eschewing publicity, her reticence over Gardner's courting of the media and concerns over his embroidering of their practice led to the conflict that Gardner frequently alluded to in his accounts of his dealings with 'the witches'. As Ronald Hutton has charted, her involvement with Gardner and with modern Pagan witchcraft had drawn to a close by 1958.[62]

The other individuals we know to have been involved at this time, practising witchcraft alongside Gardner, were Barbara and George Vickers, who circled alongside Gardner and Edith Woodford-Grimes at Bricket Wood and conceivably established a 'Northern Coven' in Cheshire. Their practice alongside, and within, Gardner's coven seems to have fizzled out by the end of 1954, while their involvement with modern witchcraft terminated, abruptly, in the spring of 1956, as Barbara abjured Paganism and was reconciled with Roman Catholicism.[63]

---

[61] Hutton, *Triumph of the Moon*, pp. 220–222; P. Heselton, *In Search of the New Forest Coven*, (Milton Keynes: Fenix Flames Publishing Ltd., 2020), pp. 156, 252–253, 255–256, 258, 262–263.

[62] Hutton, *Triumph of the Moon*, pp. 221–222. It was worth recognising, here, Prof Hutton's sensitivity and sense of professional ethics. At the time of writing the first edition of *The Triumph of the Moon*, in 1999, he respected Edith Woodford-Grimes' desire for privacy, together with that of her family, occluding her identity and referring to her only by her witch-name as 'Dafo'. By the time of the second edition, in 2019, her name had been so widely published in other accounts of Gardner and modern witchcraft that such discretion had been rendered pointless.

[63] Heselton, *Witchfather*, Vol. 2, pp. 403–409.

Accordingly, we have a cast of three known individuals who stood as 'the witches', alongside Gardner, at the fountainhead of modern Paganism. Of these, Edith Woodford-Grimes was the most significant and intellectually important. Gardner's used quotations from practising witches throughout the book to reveal something of their ideas, ideals, and experience. There is no need to dismiss these as simple fictions; indeed, they are very likely to have been rooted in the beliefs and practices of this small group of friends but as with all religions the animating spirit was deeply personal, mystical as opposed to empirical, and idealist as opposed to materialist. One of the strengths of the book, alongside the warmth and generosity of its discursiveness, was its intent to provide an insider's view of an otherwise hidden people. In this context and given that Gardner had been keen to frame the witches within the modernism of the jazz age as 'bright young things', it seems incongruous that he was also prepared to envisage the decay and final flickering-out of witchcraft. 'I think', he wrote, that:

> we must say good-bye to the witch. The cult is doomed, I am afraid, partly because of modern conditions, housing shortage, the smallness of modern families, and chiefly by education.[64]

Yet, Gardner knew that nothing was more attractive than the romantic attachment to a safely dead cause, whether reflected in the Celtic Twilight, or in the pages of *Witchcraft Today*. Say that something is lost, and there will be those who wish to find it. Indeed, the promise of growth and renewal lay in the conclusion of the passage with the note that nothing had, as yet, replaced witchcraft's 'greatest gifts' of 'peace, joy and content'.[65]

This said, witchcraft, as Gardner was keen to point out, did not set out to proselytise and 'was, and is, not a cult for everybody'.[66] He retained the idea of the organised 'witch cult' from Margaret Murray but, in almost every other respect, thoroughly revised and shifted the image of the witch, and her craft, into new territory. Of greatest significance was his removal of the Devil from witchcraft. No one else had sought to do this. Margaret Murray had maintained his dark presence at the heart of her vision of the structure of Scottish covens, while Jules Michelet (1798–1874) formulated a radiant vision of *The Witch* an archetype of womanhood and the people, tied to French soil, that alternated between outrage at the cruelty of the Catholic Church and Inquisition, and the acceptance that a kernel of Satanism operated within the craft. Gardner's genius lay in his ability in *Witchcraft Today* to strip away the darkness – the claims of the demonologists of blood sacrifices, ritual murders, curses and poisonings – to

---

[64] Gardner, *Witchcraft Today,* pp. 45, 117, 129.   [65] Gardner, *Witchcraft Today,* p. 129.
[66] Gardner, *Witchcraft Today,* pp. 29, 30.

reveal the witch as woman, healer, leader, and victim. The nine million deaths that he, again, emphasised in an immediate parallel for a post-war readership with the mechanised horrors of the *Shoah*, were guiltless and a stain upon the conscience of Europeans. Redress was to be found in a lasting toleration of a living, functioning, craft. 'The few remaining members of the cult,' he wrote, 'dived underground and have remained secretive ever since. They are happy practising their lovely old rites ... All they desire is peace.'[67]

In a similar fashion, Gardner overhauled the understanding of ceremonial magic, and replaced it with something altogether rougher, readier, and egalitarian. 'The English witches' method is entirely different', he declared, for they 'believe the power is within themselves and exudes from their bodies. It would be dissipated were it not for the circle cast ... to keep power in, and not, as magicians usually use it, to keep the spirits out. A witch can and does move freely in and out of the circle when she wishes'.[68] Here, importantly, Gardner does two things. Firstly, he distinguishes the feminised witch, as opposed to the male magus, as the one possessing the insight and power in the realms of magic; and secondly, he once again inverts the established view of circle casting, honing power within the individual as opposed to externalising it through the operation of external, demonic, forces.

The 'witch cult', therefore, appears as a universalist, matriarchal religion, stemming from the hunter gatherers of the Stone Age but eminently capable of adaption to new ideas and conditions, such as the cosmology of Ancient Egypt or the Mysteries of Classical Rome. It is non-doctrinal (witches, Gardner tells us, possess 'no books on theology'), populated by intelligent and venturesome people, and holds a belief in reincarnation.[69] The outlines of a religious praxis were clearly delineated, with accounts of the witch's tools and regalia, feasts of cakes and ale, circle casting, coven structure, the timing of festivals, dancing, the importance of poetry, and ritual and initiatory practices. While what became known as *The Book of Shadows* was alluded to as a collection of 'the witch law: [that] everyone must copy what they will from another, but no old writings may be kept. As everyone is apt to alter things slightly, modernizing the language and making other changes, it is impossible to fix the date when it became current'.[70] Here we can detect Gardner covering his traces, making an attempt to historicise 'witch law' seem pointless and doomed to failure. However, hidden in plain sight is the sense that his grimoire is a constantly evolving and entirely personal work that is both practical and inspirational, side-stepping prescribed doctrines and formulas. What Gardner was working with, at least in the 1940s, was thin

---

[67] Gardner, *Witchcraft Today,* p. 30. [68] Gardner, *Witchcraft Today,* p. 47.
[69] Gardner, *Witchcraft Today,* p. 40. [70] Gardner, *Witchcraft Today,* p. 52.

material, largely based upon the texts contained within the *Key of Solomon* and the rituals of the Golden Dawn, but capable of adaptation, expansion, and exploration. Viewed from this perspective, subsequent reductionist attempts at textual analysis seem misplaced as Gardner was interested in personal, and group, experience and not, as *Witchcraft Today* makes plain, the establishment of a credo.

Alongside the lineaments of that which would become known as Wicca, Gardner digressed into lengthy discussions of the heterodoxy and fall of the Knights Templar (in order to establish a link between the Order and the survival of elements of high magic within Freemasonry) and less successful attempts to graft fairy lore and tales of an elusive pygmy race onto his vision of witchcraft. This latter endeavour owed its inspiration to W.Y. Evans Wentz (1878–1965), a friend and colleague of W.B. Yeats and Carl Jung, whose *Fairy-Faith in the Celtic Countries* sought to systematise accounts of the fae into a coherent pattern of belief across Ireland, Scotland, Cornwall, Brittany, and the Isle of Man, that stressed reincarnation, a form of initiatory practice, and the existence of a pygmy people driven by later invaders to the margins of Europe.[71] The appeal of this academic thesis, published just prior to the Great War, was immediate to Gardner and chimed with his encounters with some of the indigenous peoples he had encountered in Malaya and Borneo. Unsurprisingly, however, these esoteric themes achieved no great foothold within Wicca.

Published in November 1954 and despite what were, at best, lukewarm reviews even in the occult press, *Witchcraft Today* became a publishing success, selling extremely well across the English-speaking world. By April 1958, it was calculated than some 5,500 copies had been purchased with its popularity spreading to North America, Australia, New Zealand, and, to a lesser extent, subsequently to Germany, the Nordic countries, and the Netherlands.[72] Relatively late in life, after several flops and false starts, Gardner found himself a literary success whose ideas began to circulate across the globe.

A follow-up volume, *The Meaning of Witchcraft,* was published in 1959 that attempted to capitalise upon his gains and refine his vision. Though 'Wica' had been introduced in the pages of *Witchcraft Today* to designate a collective of '"wise people", who practise the age-old rites', it was *The Meaning of Witchcraft* that served to settle the term (soon reworked as Wicca by journalists through phonetic spelling and by 1960s Pagans keen to align it with its Anglo-Saxon etymology) as the definition of this distinctive form of Pagan

---

[71] W. Y. Evans Wentz, *The Fairy-Faith in Celtic Countries* (Oxford: Oxford University Press, 1911).
[72] T. Greenfield (ed.), *Witchcraft Today – 60 Years on*, (Winchester, Great Britain & Washington, USA: Moon Books, 2014), p. 16.

witchcraft.[73] As such, it was quickly lodged within the public consciousness and became associated with the practice of the craft, as opposed to its membership. Gardner seems to have alighted upon it from an entry in *Chambers's Dictionary of Scots-English* denoting an individual to be 'wise' and considered it appropriate as it re-enforced Hugh Ross Williamson's conception of witchcraft as being no more, and no less, than 'the Craft of the Wise'.[74] This nomenclature then gradually but effectively replaced the previous styling of the 'witch cult', removing a somewhat pejorative term and its unintended links to authoritarian religious sects, and with it a barrier to the spread of revived witchcraft.

Drier, and lacking the immediacy and essential charm of *Witchcraft Today*, the book sought to promote Gardner's role as an anthropologist; attempted to synthesise his reading into a mosaic portrait of magic in all its hues and varieties; and to defend the freedoms won in 1951 from calls for legislative review and further persecution. The use of lengthy quotations from contemporary press articles, and the adoption of a more polemical tone, may reflect the contribution of Doreen Valiente who helped edit some portions of the book for publication.

The *Meaning of Witchcraft* did, however, create an ambiance suggesting that the 'Old Gods' were, indeed, still there: waiting amongst the woods, the streams, and hedgerows, to be rediscovered by us, just like Kipling's Wayland or Puck. If industrialised man had forgotten all about them, then they had not forgotten, or forsaken, him. 'The great persecutions could not kill' Wicca, Gardner wrote:

> because the spirit of wonder dwells in it. Its roots are set in the Ancient Magic, with its secrets of joy and terror which stir the blood and enliven the soul … in spite of all it survives; because there exists, even in the Welfare State, a spirit of romance, a love of the spice of life, and a dislike of smug respectability.[75]

Gardner's witch was, therefore, very much a rebel, linked to the Greenwood of Robin Hood, and while 'Ceremonial magic was a pursuit of "clerks" and noblemen; the witch belonged essentially to the people'.[76] Furthermore, witchcraft was defined as 'a system involving both magic and religion' and that magic, itself, was an entirely practical (but not transactional) affair, as the witch was forbidden to accept money for her endeavours, and her method of working

---

[73] Gardner, *Witchcraft Today*, pp. 102–103.
[74] Hutton, *Triumph of the Moon*, p. 249; Ross Williamson, *The Silver Bowl*, pp. 50–51.
[75] Gardner, *The Meaning of Witchcraft*, p. 257.
[76] Gardner, *The Meaning of Witchcraft*, p. 115.

was simply understood as 'the art of getting results'.[77] Wicca was 'a moon cult' celebrating the 'four great Sabbats [of] Candlemass, May Eve, Lammas, and Halloween', together with the equinoxes and solstices, 'making the Eight Ritual Occasions'.[78] This sacralisation of nature had its roots in Druidry, as well in Margaret Murray's attempts to codify witchcraft practices, and emphasised Wicca's receptiveness to the changing seasons, its preference for rural as opposed to urban settings (even if the great majority of its practitioners were town dwellers), its concern for ecology, and its attunement towards the rhythms of agricultural production and the countryside.

Alongside the celebration of nature, as a sentient force, Wicca emphasised the empowerment, rather than the subordination, of women in both its structures and conception of religious purpose and practice. This was a clear break with both the marginalisation of women within mainstream Christianity and the presiding figure of the magus in the literature and iconography of the occult revival of the nineteenth and early twentieth centuries. Indeed, save for the rapid growth of Victorian spiritualism, Wicca appears as the most fully feminised new religious movement of the modern age, and it may be thought that Gardner chose the figure of the witch as a catch-all for revived Pagan practice in order to emphasise the re-gendering of magic, the sense of the feminine as divine, and the diffusion of traditional power structures and authority through matrilineal, as opposed to patriarchal, lines. Thus, he made clear in *The Meaning of Witchcraft*, that:

> As might be expected from a moon cult, the leading part in the ceremonies is played by the High Priestess, or Maiden. She has the position of authority, and may choose any of sufficient rank in the cult to be her High Priest.[79]

For her part, the witch had 'the satisfaction of knowing that she is serving an ancient creed which she believes to be true ... a life that holds infinite possibilities, and is entirely satisfying' with the 'experience of pleasures whose very existence is unknown to the majority of people' and with knowledge 'of the ordered pattern behind apparently unrelated things' together with, perhaps most importantly of all, the conquest of fear and the setting aside of guilt.[80] Consequently, witchcraft (under the guise of Wicca) was for the first time Pagan, a vehicle for feminist and ecological expression, and no longer a product of poverty and desperation, but of hope, conscious choice, and a sense of revolt against modernity.

---

[77] Gardner, *The Meaning of Witchcraft*, pp. 21, 99.
[78] Gardner, *The Meaning of Witchcraft*, p. 19.   [79] Gardner, *The Meaning of Witchcraft*, p. 19.
[80] Gardner, *The Meaning of Witchcraft*, p. 37.

5 The Tower: Witchcraft on the Isle of Man

In the spring of 1951, Gardner boarded a plane bound for the Isle of Man. This journey and his subsequent media incarnation as 'the resident witch' at *The Folklore Centre of Superstition and Witchcraft,* at Castletown, marked a watershed in his life. He went at the invitation of the museum's owner, Cecil Williamson (1909–99), a filmmaker, former Rhodesian tobacco planter and occultist, whom Gardner had met, in 1947, at the *Atlantis* Bookshop. Yet, his role grew swiftly as he advised upon the creation and framing of the displays, lent items from his own collection and from that of the 'Southern Coven' (probably items belonging to Edith Woodford-Grimes and those used to set the scene for the 'Witch's Cottage' in Bricket Wood), and held court in the museum as guide, selling signed copies of *High Magic's Aid* to tourists. As the museum ran into difficulty, Gardner provided loans and took on the mortgage of the site, giving him financial control over the business and the ability to push for more control. It was at this point that his relationship with Williamson soured and broke down beyond repair.

Part of the rupture can be explained through a clash of personalities but, just as important, in establishing the breach were the differing visions of witchcraft owned and promoted by the two men. Williamson emphasised witchcraft's dark lustre, its curses, brutal suppression, and demonic outrages, concentrating upon ceremonial magic; while Gardner stressed the healings, blessings, survivals, and liberating mysteries of village level, popular – but far from populist – magic. Consequently, their visions came into conflict and arguments broke out over the manner of display of the artefacts lent by Gardner and Woodford-Grimes, and Williamson's failure to deliver on a promise to house them within their own room at the museum. Gardner's exasperation is apparent in a letter to Williamson, written on 1 August 1953, stating:

> If you will only tell me clearly what you are aiming at, possibly I could help you, but it must be true. I will not co-operate in making a Denis [*sic*] Wheatley, Montague Summers pack of lies.[81]

A far more practical response, which demonstrated Gardner's capacity for ruthlessness, came with his move to increase the interest rate on Williamson's mortgage and, then, call in his loans. Facing financial ruin, Williamson attempted to play for time, set up a torture exhibition in the funfair outside Douglas, and attempted to secure a new home for his museum at the fishing port of Peel. When these initiatives fell through, he packed away his collections and

---

[81] Museum of Witchcraft & Magic, Boscastle, G.30, letter from G. Gardner to C. Williamson, 1 August 1953, ff.1–2.

Cambridge Elements

Magic

William Pooley
University of Bristol

William Pooley is Senior Lecturer in Modern History at the University of Bristol and co-editor of the forthcoming *Cambridge Companion to the Witch*. He is the author of *Body and Tradition in Nineteenth-century France: Félix Arnaudin and the Moorlands of Gascony* (2019) and co-author of the CUP Element *Creative Histories of Witchcraft: France, 1790-1940* (2022). His next book is a history of witchcraft in France from the French Revolution to World War Two.

About the Series

Elements in Magic aims to restore the study of magic, broadly defined, to a central place within culture: one which it occupied for many centuries before being set apart by changing discourses of rationality and meaning. Understood as a continuing and potent force within global civilisation, magical thinking is imaginatively approached here as a cluster of activities, attitudes, beliefs and motivations which include topics such as alchemy, astrology, divination, exorcism, the fantastical, folklore, haunting, supernatural creatures, necromancy, ritual, spirit possession and witchcraft.

Cambridge Elements

Magic

Elements in the Series

The War on Witchcraft: Andrew Dickson White, George Lincoln Burr, and the Origins of Witchcraft Historiography
Jan Machielsen

Witchcraft and the Modern Roman Catholic Church
Francis Young

'Ritual Litter' Redressed
Ceri Houlbrook

Representing Magic in Modern Ireland: Belief, History, Culture
Andrew Sneddon

Creative Histories of Witchcraft: France, 1790–1940
Poppy Corbett, Anna Kisby Compton and William G. Pooley

Witchcraft and Paganism in Midcentury Women's Detective Fiction
Jem Bloomfield

The Gut: A Black Atlantic Alimentary Tract
Elizabeth Pérez

The Donkey King: Asinine Symbology in Ancient and Medieval Magic
Emily K. Selove

Amulets in Magical Practice
Jay Johnston

Staging Witchcraft before the Law: Skepticism, Performance as Proof, and Law as Magic in Early Modern Witch Trials
Julie Stone Peters

Lowcountry Conjure Magic: Historical Archaeology on a Plantation Slave Quarter
Sharon K. Moses

Gerald Gardner and the Creation of Wicca
John Callow

A full series listing is available at: www.cambridge.org/EMGI

left the Isle for good in March 1955, nursing an abiding (and understandable) grudge against Gardner, and founding new witchcraft museums at Bourton-on-the-Water, in Gloucestershire, and at Boscastle, in Cornwall.[82] The latter establishment continues to thrive to this day.

Gardner was left with little more than a shell of a building, but undeterred, he renamed the site *The Museum of Magic and Witchcraft* (it was also more popularly known as *The Witches' Mill* on account of the ruined windmill tower at centre of the complex) and began to restock it with his own collections, in time for opening at the start of the tourist season in 1954. Though often overlooked in his history of modern witchcraft, the Manx museum came to play a significant role in the last decade of Gardner's life and in the development of Wicca. Gardner's official biography foregrounded the museum as one of the three key strands of his magical career. The first was 'the founding practise' of Wicca; the second was 'the academic establishment of the reality of the religion' (through *Witchcraft Today* and *The Meaning of Witchcraft*); and the third, 'the last and perhaps the greatest part seems to be the foundation and maintenance of his collection of magical and witchcraft relics'.[83] The reasoning behind this claim was based upon the premise that:

> The heritage of witchcraft is largely unseen ... But the museum stands, in material form, not only as a memorial to the martyrs of the Craft. It is above all something which can be seen and understood, by people at three levels of perception. The general public can obtain an understanding of what magic and witchcraft mean by visiting the Isle of Man. Scholars can send their queries there, can come to study, can exchange ideas and correlate research – because of the Museum. And, to the members of the Wica, this can be a symbol of their beliefs, and a permanent home for some of their regalia.[84]

Gardner was concerned about his legacy and had, in the words of Fred Lamond (an initiate of the Bricket Wood Coven), the air of being 'an old man in a hurry'.[85] This revealed itself in everything from his bicycle rides across Castletown, undertaken at breakneck speed and with scant regard for traffic signals, to his plans for overhauling the museum displays, the building of a dancehall, with a sprung floor, on the side of the mill complex, and the pace of his writing and media schedule. Gardner wrote both *Witchcraft Today* and *The Meaning of Witchcraft* while on the Isle, and the themes of local witch trials and folk lore permeate the texts with a strong sense of the history and mythology

---

[82] R. White, *The Witches House: Cecil Williamson and his Museums* (no place: Antenna Publications, 2025), pp. 118, 124–125, 132.
[83] Bracelin, *Witch*, p. 217.   [84] Bracelin, *Witch*, p. 217.
[85] Hutton, *Triumph of the Moon*, p. 250; F. Lamond, *Fifty Years of Wicca* (Sutton Mallet: Green Magic, 2004), pp. 17–18.

of the indigenous, Gaelic-speaking, people. We are told of the use of Manx charms and of the examples kept in his museum; of the apparition of the spectral Black Dog (or 'Moddey Dhoo') at Peel Castle; of the deeds of the Sea God, Manannan Mac Lir; of encounters at the Fairy Bridge (where 'themselves' or the fae needed to be saluted); of recent archaeological digs and discoveries; and of the use of the Lord Bishops' ecclesiastical prison and of the methods of detecting, and prosecuting, witches on Man, culminating in the witch-burning of Margaret Quane and her son, John Cubbon, in Castletown in 1617.[86]

For Gardner, the witch-burning and persecution of Margaret Quane became emblematic of the European witch trials of the sixteenth and seventeenth centuries and the emotive centrepiece of his museum complex. He painted the scene many times over, fashioned a beautifully intricate boxed diorama showing the execution, installed a commemorative plaque over a pre-existing monument at the reputed site of the burnings, and through his writings championed Margaret Quane and her son as being members of an underground witch religion, or fertility cult. Significantly, he overhauled the memorial to the victims of 'superstition' created by Cecil Williamson for the museum. Originally, this had been conceived as a modernist, polished stone sphere: a form of conceptual as opposed to representational art. Upon Williamson's departure, the installation (realised in painted plywood as opposed to stone) seems to have been lost or destroyed.[87] However, Gardner returned to this earlier theme of the need to memorialise suffering, radically transforming Williamson's notions of suffering and victimhood and linking them, explicitly, to the practice of Wicca. Witchcraft, in his eyes, was not the product of base superstition; and the witches were not the perpetrators of the crime (which could be inferred from Williamson's formulation) but its guiltless victims. Therefore, the paradigm shifted dramatically as Gardner created his own monument to the 'martyrs of the craft' and the 'nine million victims' of the European trials.

His monument was, in some ways, far more modest than Williamson's (Figure 2). It consisted of his own painting of Margaret Quane staring imploring out of the flames of the pyre, with a dedicatory inscription, framed separately, below it. Mounted upon a plywood pillar and draped in black velvet, it served as a movable display that could be photographed out-of-doors, as well as occupying pride of place in the museum's upstairs galleries. It was also intended to be interactive and capable of eliciting an emotional response from museum visitors. An 'eternal flame' burned beside it, and a chalice was set at its base, which could be used either as a container for offerings or as an incense burner,

---

[86] Gardner, *Witchcraft Today,* pp. 35, 39, 50–51, 56, 57–58, 68–69, 122, 132–133; Gardner, *Meaning of Witchcraft,* pp. 13, 14, 34, 169
[87] White, *The Witches House,* p. 97.

Figure 2 The memorial to the 'Nine Million' victims of witch persecution, painted by Gardner c.1954–56. At its centre is the portrayal of Margaret Quayne's burning, in 1617, at Castletown, Isle of Man.

honouring the sacrifice and suffering not just of one Manx woman but of all the reputed nine million dead. As such, it was a powerful, yet tender, reminder of individuals who lacked a resting place, whose stories had largely been forgotten, and whose reputations had been systematically trampled underfoot.

The experience of Manx witchcraft was, thus, foregrounded within the nascent history of Wicca. This could also be seen in Gardner's fashioning of an eldritch backstory for his museum as 'the Witches' Mill', where 'the famous Arbory witches' practised their arts and, after 1848, used its ruins as their 'dancing ground ... screened ... from the wind and from prying eyes'.[88] The reality, however, was somewhat different. The mill was built in the nineteenth

---

[88] G. B. Gardner, *The Museum of Magic and Witchcraft: The Story of the Famous Witches Mill at Castletown, Isle of Man* (Tunbridge Wells: The Witches Mill / Photocrom Co. Ltd., n/d c.1958), p. 5.

century, as opposed to the seventeenth as Gardner had claimed; there had, indeed, been a fire which gutted the windmill in 1848, but thereafter the site remained a bustling centre of agricultural production and small-scale industry. It was a spot, on a main road, hardly given to secrecy. Furthermore, Gardner took the term 'Arbory witches' from the work of David Craine, on individual cases of witchcraft in the parishes adjoining Castletown. These were not linked to the mill site, and there is no evidence to suggest anything resembling a group practice or coven structure in the trial records.

What is clear from the recent studies by Stephen Miller and Professor Jim Sharpe is that the Isle had been gripped by accusations surrounding a number of women folk-charmers, in 1616–17, who were targeted for practising malevolent witchcraft. Long-standing local grudges against a troublesome and frequently drunken extended family, when allied to weak local government and the importation of Anglo-Scottish witch theory, were more than enough to see Margaret Quane and her illegitimate son charged and burned at the stake. However, the polarisation of island society that accompanied the trial, together with revulsion at the savagery of their deaths, ensured that once the local elites reasserted their governance, there was to be no such repeat of the panic, with Manx justices and juries proving extremely reluctant to prosecute for the crime of witchcraft.

Gardner's vision of Margaret Quane as a Pagan martyr, who had died in order to secure the good of the people and the harvest, is – just like his claims for the 'Arbory witches' – unsupported by any archival evidence. In a similar fashion, claims by contemporary Pagan writers that Manx covens survived and even flourished on the Isle, prior to the arrival of Gardner, are pure fantasy, stemming from a combination of wishful thinking and the tendency to take the wealth of imaginative Victorian fiction, stemming from the Celtic revival, at face value. Williamson had desperately sought out Manx witches and charmers for his museum, only to be disappointed; and his turn to Gardner to fill this void was the very thing that had precipitated Gerald's first visit to, and engagement with, the Isle in July 1951. Gardner's own failure to find practising witches on the Isle of Man was frequently highlighted, with gentle amusement, in the pages of the Manx press and he was forced to hire an Irish waitress, May Daily, in order to perform the role of an aspiring witch for an early photoshoot. The simple, unvarnished, fact was that the establishment of the museum, coupled with the publication of *Witchcraft Today* and *The Meaning of Witchcraft*, provided a case of practice being called into being by art.

Gardner claimed that 'Witchcraft doesn't pay for broken windows!' but the record of the Museum of Magic and Witchcraft, from 1954 to 1964, was one of financial success and great public interest.[89] On an island that was not otherwise noted for its cultural and social permissiveness, a key component in enabling toleration to flourish was Gardner's framing of witchcraft itself. He made generous use of his spurious academic title, enjoyed his rendering as the Isle's resident 'Witch-doctor' in the pages of the local press (playing upon both the Manx tradition of cunning folk and the operation of indigenous magic in the developing world), and stressed his expertise as a professional anthropologist. His vivid personality and public profile (through TV, radio, and press interviews) meant that he was well-liked and thought of, often with pride, as a local celebrity. He was affectionately recalled as 'the Old Master', 'the Grand Old Man', or more simply as 'a nice old boy' by those who had known him, on the Isle, in their youth. Whereas Alexander Cannon, operating out of a grand house in the north of the island had, from the 1930s onwards, stressed the sinister lure of high, Eastern magic, unappreciable to all but a small social elite, Gardner's evocation of a beneficent, low magic, available to all rooted in the Manx countryside, appeared as being, at worst, innocuous, and more generally as helpful or personally empowering. At the same time, Gardner's healthy and homespun version of witchcraft served to dull the cankerous memory of the 'Dalby Spook', a talking mongoose (part poltergeist, part shape-changing familiar spirit) who had haunted, and ultimately ruined, the life of the teenage daughter of a Manx farmer, during the 1930s.[90] In this manner, an altogether different, and highly novel, view of the practice of witchcraft appeared timely and was afforded the liberty, or licence, to take shape on the Isle.

This reshaping took place primarily through the displays in the museum galleries (Figure 3). Eventually, eighteen display cases sat on three floors in the old granary building. There were recreations of Palaeolithic cave paintings, and the foliate masks of Green Men that (thanks to the works of Lady Raglan and Margaret Murray) appeared to suggest pagan continuity and survival, while a charmed cradle was said, if rocked by a young woman, to promise fertility and a swift and easy childbirth. Manuscripts from the Order of the Golden Dawn and a charter from Crowley sat alongside black scrying mirrors (that came from Victorian fairgrounds) and displays devoted to fortune telling, the Tarot, and Rosicrucianism. However, the centrepieces of the museum were two tableaus that sought to juxtapose high and low magic, through the recreation of, respectively, 'a Magician's Study' and 'a Witch's Cottage' (Figure 4).[91]

The difficulty remained in the exposition of a hidden religion. Popular, as opposed to elite, magical tools had not survived. Thus, the most direct way of

---
[89] Gardner, *Witchcraft Today*, p. 18.
[90] See: C. Josiffe, *Gef! The Strange Tale of an Extra-Special Talking Mongoose* (London: strange Attractor Press, 2017 rpt. 2021).
[91] Gardner, *Museum of Magic and Witchcraft*, p. 11.

Figure 3 The new exhibition galleries on the upper floor of the Museum of Magic and Witchcraft, Castletown, c.1960. Seven fresh display cases, devoted to the practice of ritual magic, frame a magic circle and a mill wheel, repurposed to denote the ritual turning of the year.

Figure 4 Gerald Gardner in the 'Witch's Cottage' tableau at his museum, c.1960. He is surrounded by the witches' tools and sits just outside the arc of the ritual space inscribed upon the floor.

making good the gaps in the knowledge of Wicca was to draw upon the expertise of Gardner, himself. He trailed the tantalising suggestion in his guidebook that:

> the remains of the original pre-Christian religion of Western Europe, and its followers possessed traditional knowledge and beliefs which had been handed down by word of mouth for generations ... the cult has never died. Some remnants of it still exist to this day, and the Director of this Museum has been initiated into a British witch coven.[92]

As a result, the museum was deluged with postal enquiries, on a daily basis, asking for everything from help with spells to win the pools, to attract a lover, to secure health or professional advancement, to insights into Wicca and requests for initiation. These latter requests were prioritised with Gardner employing successive managers at *The Witches' Mill* to act as his correspondence secretaries, sifting the mail, and following up with advice to would-be initiates and, often, putting them in contact with the nearest of Gardner's functioning covens. In this way, Arnold and Patricia Crowther would be initiated in Castletown, in June 1960, Ray Buckland was initiated in Perth, in November 1963, and a working coven was established on the Isle, operating out of the barn attached to Gardner's home and, after hours, on the top floor of his museum.

This Manx coven had a fluctuating membership but appears to have attracted individuals from all classes and walks of life. Leading Manx professionals and opinion formers circled alongside housewives, craftsmen, and mechanics. H.L. Dor, the dominant figure in the Manx newspaper industry from the 1950s to the 1970s, provided vital exposure for Wicca through the pages of *Fate* (a popular esoteric journal) and his commercial presses, operating out of the *Isle of Man Times* building in Douglas. These would publish Denys Teare's *Folk-Doctor's Island* (in 1963) which would include a highly sympathetic account of a meeting with Gardner, and *The Witches Speak* (in 1965), the first account of Wicca by Arnold and Paricia Crowther. Moreover, Dor's esoteric novel, *Killers from the Common Market*, published in 1963, revolved around the magical ambiance of the Isle of Man and the workings of Gardner's coven. Indeed, Gardner, himself, appears in the novel's closing pages providing its denouement, and in a manner that emphasised his personal kindness and possession of a preternatural, second sight. Of equal note is Dor's account of a healing ritual worked by the coven, whereby a young High Priestess stepped naked into the circle:

> alive, yet transmuted, a person, yet a symbol, the pure archetype of all dreams ... he saw Mrs. Crellin drawing the Circle on the floor, all upturned buttocks and blithe unselfconsciousness. Her daughter hovered on the edge, a young sprite at the dawn of wonder. Wladimir [a former Polish resistance

---
[92] Gardner, *Museum of Magic and Witchcraft*, p. 8.

fighter, tortured and blinded by the Nazis] sat in the middle, having adopted automatically the Yogi lotus position with upturned palms of the feet, which he used for meditation in prison ... Then they began to turn. Their fingers were only touching at intervals. The movement was hardly greater than that of a sleep-walker, but already a tremendous contrary speed started to build up, revolving against their chests in the opposite sense to their own. It was like the operating of a dynamo ... And this rush of electricity on their bare skins, made their bodies glow with the warmth of sunbathing and the phosphorescence of swimming in a tropical sea and something more, as if the power was being drawn from within themselves, yet blended with that emanating from the others ... But suddenly the inner circle, revolving against them, broke and all the power drained away towards the middle, gathering itself over Wladimir and plunged [healing and charging him like a central dynamo].[93]

Though fictionalised, this is probably the best working account we are likely to get of the practice of Gardner's Manx coven, focusing as it does, upon the importance of raising power for healing practices, through group work (Figure 5). Once again, there is a progressive undercurrent with Wicca coming to the aid of the oppressed and setting itself in conscious opposition to Nazism.

Figure 5 A Witches' Dance: probably the first depiction of a Wiccan rite, that appeared as an illustration to the novel, *Killers from the Common Market*, published in 1962.

---

[93] H. L. Dor, *Killers from the Common Market* (Douglas: Times Press Ltd. / The Island Development Company Ltd., n/d but 1963), pp. 83–84.

At the same time, Idries Shah (1924–96), a prolific author, Sufi mystic, and ceremonial magician, had settled on the island. He needed a patron, a source of steady income, and an intellectual and magical partner. Gardner, whom he had met through Jack Bracelin in London, appeared to fit the bill perfectly. For his part, Gardner needed a capable biographer who could lay to rest the slanders being levelled at him by his would-be rival, Charles Cardell. The result was the brief flowering of a friendship and a creative synthesis that brought Wicca (with its emphasis upon popular Western magic) together with a progressive strain of Sufism that looked towards parallel magical practices drawn from across the Middle East. Gardner was greatly impressed by Shah's studies of *Oriental Magic* (1956) and *The Secret Law of Magic* (1957), which acted, respectively, as an exploration of Jewish, Arabian, North African, Indian, and Chinese magical practices; and as a collection of grimoires drawn predominantly from early modern European sources that had been freshly translated, edited, and annotated for a twentieth-century audience.[94] Shah thus provided a form of magical praxis that Gardner found riveting and which began to influence, and find expression in, the evolution of Wicca.

Through Shah, Gardner had come to a greater appreciation of the work of Robert Graves and contact was made between the two men and the author of *The White Goddess,* over the winter of 1960–61. The parallels between their work on the theme of the divine feminine and the universality of a mother goddess were both immediate and striking, and Graves had read (and would later favourably review) *Witchcraft Today.* Accordingly, Gardner and Shah joined Graves, in Palma, in January 1961. The substance of their meeting was not recorded but it went sufficiently well for Graves to invite them back to his home, in Deya, a week later.

However, it was Shah who had caught Graves' attention and imagination. Gardner had failed to impress and was quietly, if courteously, dropped from their company. Consequently, the meetings in Mallorca represent a watershed in the early history of Wicca. The potential offered by Gardner's 'Witch Cult' had undoubtedly exerted a glamour upon Graves, and writing two years later, he ventured that:

> the craft seems healthy enough ... and growing fast. It now only needs some gifted mystic to come forward, decently reclothe it, and restore its original hunger for wisdom.[95]

---

[94] I. Shah, *Oriental Magic* (London: Rider & Co. Ltd., 1956); I. Shah, *The Secret Lore of Magic: Books of the Sorcerers* (London: Frederick Muller Ltd., 1957).
[95] R. Graves, *The Crane Bag and Other Disputed Subjects*, (London: Cassell, 1969), p. 224.

However, Gardner's levity and his lack of philosophical underpinning, which might have been secured through a fuller understanding of Classical pagan sources, rendered Wicca 'insufficient' and a matter of no more than 'Fun and games'.[96] Instead, Graves suggested that Shah might be the one to fuse a revived Paganism with the magical traditions of the Ancient World. As it was, Shah demurred, and the result of the long-standing friendship between him and Graves did not result in the reforging of Wicca but in a joint exploration of mystical Islam, the world of the Jinns, and of the *Rubaiyat of Omar Khayyam*.

Effectively, and somewhat clinically, Shah had exchanged one master for another, and Gardner was left to return home to promote his newly published biography. Work on the book had stalled and had been taken over by Jack Bracelin who managed, within a matter of weeks, to weld the fragmentary notes and interviews into a coherent and engaging life of Gardner that showcased his vision of Wicca. Published shortly before his departure for the Mediterranean, *Witch* undoubtedly portrays Gardner as he wished to be seen by posterity and provides an invaluable primary source for his life, sense of priorities, and ideas. Without it, it would be difficult, if not impossible, to reconstruct Gardner's early life and cross-cultural engagement. Shah's influence, in foregrounding Gardner's interest in indigenous religions, was key in this respect, and it is reasonable to suggest that the bulk of the work, leading up to Gardner's visit to Cyprus in 1938, was largely his work.[97] This explains the relative brevity with which the genesis and early history of Wicca is afforded, as Bracelin took up the task of completing the work. That which should have been central, appears almost as a coda – though a satisfying and triumphant one – to the biographical narrative. As a result, the text is far more uneven than it might have been and lacked the distinctive impact of esoteric Islam that Shah would have woven into it. Bracelin's portion of the book, from Chapter 13 onwards, placed a greater impact upon Gardner's direct speech and served to throw the spotlight firmly upon his evolving conception of Wicca as a 'rediscovered' nature religion. Though to be treated with caution, the book is far less driven by ego and hyperbole than many (if not most) exercises in self-published, official biography. As such, it stands alongside *Witchcraft Today* and *The Meaning of Witchcraft* as one of Wicca's foundational documents and is an account that is redolent with the affection and esteem that Bracelin felt for the old man and enriched by Shah's knowledge of Eastern mysticism and systems of high magic.

If Gardner's encounter with Sufism had terminated abruptly with the severing of his friendship with Shah and his opportunity to find mainstream publishers

---

[96] Graves, *The Crane Bag and Other Disputed Subjects*, p. 224.
[97] P. Heselton, 'A Tale of Two Biographers: The Making of Gerald Gardner – Witch', *The Cauldron*, no. 137, (August 2010), pp. 36–39.

for his work vanished along with Robert Graves; then he rapidly and adeptly repositioned himself for North American audiences, finding an outlet for Wicca in the pages of *New Dimensions,* a well-produced magazine newly launched by Llewellyn, the leading publisher of occult books in the United States. The focus of modern Paganism upon initiatory lineages has tended to reduce accounts of the introduction of Wicca to North America to the establishment of a coven in Long Island by Ray and Rosemary Buckland. Yet, the strenuous promotion of Wicca within the pages of *New Dimensions* in 1963–64 was just as significant. This began with the publication of articles by Patricia Crowther, as the High Priestess of the Sheffield Coven, providing an overview of revived witchcraft that dismissed demonology, recounted historic witch persecutions at the hands of the Christian church, and laid stress upon Wicca's coven structure, belief in reincarnation, roots in tribal magic, and efficacy in the modern world. This was followed by an article distinguishing between the high magic of ceremonial magicians and the low, or popular, magic of Wicca.

Her husband, Arnold, also published in the journal but in a rationalist context, as a stage magician recounting tales of the survival of African indigenous beliefs among Sotho troops during the Second World War. Yet, it was the female agency and voice that counted within Wicca, and Gardner, at last, had a bright and charismatic High Priestess, who looked the part, and was willing to publicly self-define as a witch in order to help promote his ideas. Wicca was, for the first time, more than just Gerald Gardner and began to assume the lineaments of a movement.

Gardner understood this and rather than recapitulating the High Priestess' vision, he moved onto new ground that reflected both his ability as a storyteller and his growing interest in the folklore of the Isle of Man. One of these, the story of 'George' (his familiar spirit and house gremlin), was published in *New Dimensions* in January 1964, and reveals Gardner in fine and charmingly self-deprecating form. Gentle and warm in tone, it played with some of the established tropes of Manx folklore, with the gremlin following Gardner across the sea from England and establishing a friendship with the Moddey Dhoo (or 'Black Dog' of Peel Castle), roughing up the local seagulls, and finding the faeries of the Isle conceited and stand-offish.[98]

It also revealed the focus of Gardner's writings as he made copious (though repetitive and badly ordered) notes on Manx witchcraft and folklore that were presumably intended to form the basis of a series of articles and a new book. Only the first article on 'Witchcraft on the Isle of Man' would appear, in

---

[98] G. B. Gardner, 'The Truth About George', *New Dimensions*, Vol. 1 no. 5 (December 1963–January 1964), pp. 36–38.

March 1964, providing an overview of folk belief (drawn predominantly from the work of the eighteenth-century antiquarian and polemicist George Waldron) and witch trials (culled from accounts republished in the *Journal of the Manx Museum* by David Craine, from the 1940s onwards). Gardner also took the opportunity to rework his account of the 'Witches Mill', taken from his museum guide; equating the families of folk charmers on the Isle to Pagan witchcraft; and linking trial accounts of women arraigned in 1663 and 1695 to the practice of a fertility religion and ritual nudity. In summary, he offered the opinion that:

> Witches in the Isle-of-Man today follow the practices and beliefs of those in Great Britain and the Continent, that is, they worship some Celtic Gods, or possibly they worship some gods who were later taken into the Celtic religion. That is the Old European God of the next world, and the Great Mother who was probably European but with some affiliations with the near East.[99]

This provided a neat synthesis of the theories of Margaret Murray and Robert Graves, while also tying them to a form of current religious expression that was, in this case, not the product of wishful thinking or fallacy. By 1964, there were Pagan witches practising coven-based witchcraft on the Isle of Man. That they were doing so as the result of Gardner's inspiration, rather than as part of a survival from pre-history, did not matter in this context. If, at best, Wicca dated back little more than a decade in its Manx heartland, then it could be argued that there was wonder and achievement in being at the creation of a mystery religion, as opposed to its mere inheritor. The Eleusinian mysteries had had to begin somewhere and Gardner understood with every fibre of his being that the best way to promote a radical and immensely challenging project was to clothe it in the garb of conservative tradition. With covens firmly established in Castletown, Perth, Bricket Wood, South London, Sheffield and Manchester, and opportunities opening up on the East Coast of America; his books, articles, and press interviews gaining attention; and the cultural climate in the UK beginning to thaw after the reaction of the 1950s, Gardner was riding a wave of success as he prepared to leave for his annual winter cruise in November. However, he was not destined to realise his plans for a book to re-enchant the Manx nation, or even to see anything more than the proof copies of his article on witchcraft on the Isle. He died of a stroke, on 12 February 1964, while sitting on the deck of a cargo ship off the coast of Tunis, a book on magic slipping from his hands.

---

[99] G. B. Gardner, 'Witchcraft ... In the Isle of Man', *New Dimensions*, Vol. 1 no. 6, (February–March 1964), p. 9.

6 The High Priestess: Feminising the New 'Old' Religion

Gardner had given a new form of expression to what appeared to be an old magic that was capable of innovation, and which was still evolving at the time of his passing. Indeed, he entrusted sheaves of newly written rituals to his confidant, Angus Macleod, shortly before departing on his last voyage. Some of these additions (such as his spurious discovery of 'witch words' and 'laws of the craft' (which appeared just in time for him to re-enforce his authority within the Bricket Wood Coven), the emphasis upon the fae in his books, and his championing of 'the new ... Aquarian Age' gleaned late in his career from Doreen Valiente, have disappeared from the contemporary practice of Wicca.[100] Even his focus upon reincarnation has faded to the margins. Yet, the core concept of Wicca as a feminising (and increasingly feminist) religion has remained central to the movement set in motion after 1953. The paradox underlying its creation lies in his male authorship, and, consequently, there have been revisionist attempts to minimalise his role, or fictive endeavours to posit the survival of 'true' witchcraft lines, running parallel or cross-fertilising with his own.[101] Unfortunately, the precise role played by Edith Woodford-Grimes (whether as partner, muse, or original thinker) is lost in Wicca's pre-history, and with it the creative impact of the first woman to almost certainly define as a Pagan witch within it. What is clear is that Gardner, at times, deferred to her judgments, whether over the fate of the artefacts lent to Cecil Williamson's museum or the limiting of his contacts with the media. However, if we wish to posit a single female influence upon the genesis of Wicca, then one could do no better than to look to Margaret Murray. She had driven the idea of 'the witch cult' and her inspiration compelled Gardner to attempt to fashion a religion from her imaginative synthesis of history and anthropology.[102] Still, Murray's 'God of the Witches' remained a dominant male divinity, and she devoted scant time or interest to developing a goddess centred religion.

Such lacunae add to the sense of Gardner's radicalism. He deployed his privilege as a man of means to fashion a religious system that consciously aimed to empower women. His was a countercultural force far greater in impact and vision than anything else that the 'new age' professed to offer, with its success registered through its rapid shift from a male to a female leadership, and

---
[100] Gardner, *The Meaning of Witchcraft*, pp. 258–259.
[101] Heselton, *Doreen Valiente*, p. xv; R. Hutton, *The Pagan Religions of the Ancient British Isles: Their Nature and Legacy* (Oxford: Blackwell, 1991 rpt. 1993), pp. 332–333; Anon., 'Before Gardner – What?', *Pentagram: A Witchcraft Review*, no. 2, (November 1964), p. 1; R. Cochrane, 'The Craft Today', op.cit. p. 8.
[102] K. L. Sheppard, *The Life of Margaret Alice Murray: A Woman's Work in Archaeology*, (New York: Lexington Books, 2013), pp. 162, 166–175, 177.

in its continuing growth in terms of both numbers and cultural reach, across the Western World, transcending and out-pacing its original coven-based structure. This is not to claim that Gardner was anything more than a man of his times, who stressed the heteronormative in respect to magical working through sexual polarity and who can be accused of objectifying women through his writings and art.[103] Yet, in refusing to assume the mantle of the magus (the obvious route open to him through the precedents of Samuel Liddell Mathers and Aleister Crowley) he was breaking new ground in eschewing personal leadership, dominant insight, and patriarchal authority. Personal freedom, as opposed to supplication, was the cornerstone of his brand of revived Paganism, whereby 'the witch religion recognises all women as an incarnation of the Goddess, and all men as an incarnation of the God'.[104]

Wicca was a matriarchy, women had always been 'dominant in the cult practice' and, significantly within the coven, 'although woman can on occasion take man's place, man can never take woman's place'.[105] The office of High Priestess was paramount, vital in the 'Group soul', the working of magic and communion with the gods, and was to be venerated by her High Priest (as representative of the Horned God) during rites. Furthermore, the binary method of initiation (from woman to man, and man to woman) emphasised the flow of power from its female source and, in this context, it is significant that Gardner's 'origin story' of the Craft turns upon his initiation by a woman. He was always the servant as opposed to the master of the witches.

This centring of Wicca upon the insight, power, and agency of women was there from the very first in Gardner's emphasis upon the female as divine. 'It is all', he tells us, 'very simple and direct', as:

> The goddess of the witch cult is obviously the Great Mother, the giver of life, incarnate love. She rules spring, pleasure, feasting and all the delights. She was identified at a later time with other goddesses, and has a special affinity with the moon.[106]

Following this, he reveals something of the initiatory rite and the text of a charge, bearing more than a nod to Apuleius' evocation of the goddess Isis, that commands the postulant to:

> Listen to the words of the Great Mother, who of old was also called among men Artemis, Astarte, Dione, Melusine, Aphrodite and many other names. At mine altars the youth of Lacedaemon [Sparta] made due sacrifice. Once in the

---

[103] Gardner, *Witchcraft Today*, p. 115; Gardner, *The Meaning of Witchcraft*, pp. 128–130; Bourne, *Dancing with Witches*, p. 38.
[104] Gardner, *The Meaning of Witchcraft*, p. 129.   [105] Gardner, *Witchcraft Today*, pp. 33, 44.
[106] Gardner, *Witchcraft Today*, p. 42.

month, and better it be when the moon is full, meet in some secret place and adore me, who am queen of all magics ... For I am a gracious goddess, I give joy on earth, certainty, not faith, while in life; and upon death, peace unutterable, rest and the ecstasy of the goddess. Nor do I demand aught in sacrifice.[107]

This was as close as one was likely to get to a credo in a religion that consciously espoused 'no theology [and] little hierarchy', and it was one that placed women, and womanhood, at the heart of its praxis.[108] Wicca was to be 'the story of the goddess', and it was through the individual and collective endeavours of Gardner's High Priestesses that it would flourish and define itself over the next three decades, providing an outlet for the religious expression of women that was unmatched in any of the established or other new religions.[109] Long before it caught the zeitgeist of the late 1960s and Second Wave feminism, it combined sexual and personal liberation, and the absence of hierarchy and the cult of personality, with a feminised religion that attempted to own a tradition while operating within, and engaging with, modernity. Gardner had ensured that no one accepted money for their art, and with no priestly class to support, no donations to make (aside from the customary 'cakes and wine' picnic after a Circle), and no temples, premises, or offices to upkeep, Wicca exuded a sense of egalitarianism and a practice that often centred upon the suburban home as opposed to the woods or ancient ritual sites. If we look at the backgrounds of Gardner's High Priestesses we are presented with a remarkable cross-section of post-war British society. Doreen Valiente had experienced protracted periods of unemployment before working as a bookseller, shorthand typist and furniture maker; Eleanor ('Ray') Bone ran a nursing home; Lois Bourne worked as a nurse; Patricia Crowther had performed on the variety stage and was an accomplished professional actress, singer and musician; while Monique Wilson was a housewife, from a mixed French-Vietnamese background, who railed against life on a drab Perth housing estate.

Of these, Doreen Valiente (1922–99) enjoyed the highest public profile and greatest critical acclaim, having written a succession of influential books on the practice and purpose of revived witchcraft. Though her time within Gardner's coven was relatively brief (running from July 1953 to February 1957), she had a gift for writing rituals (re-working existing materials and composing new works, including the 'Charge of the Goddess' and 'The Witches' Rune'), contributing extracts from her voluminous scrapbooks of newspaper articles to the latter chapters of *The Meaning of Witchcraft*, and producing a large

---

[107] Gardner, *Witchcraft Today*, p. 42. [108] Bracelin, *Gerald Gardner: Witch*, p. 203.
[109] Gardner, *Witchcraft Today*, p. 40.

quantity of rhyming verse that sought to capture the essence of Wicca. Her publication, in 1978, of a *Book of Shadows* as the concluding part of *Witchcraft for Tomorrow* (a title that consciously played upon Gardner's account) provided a rich stimulus in the form of a 'self-help' guide to a new generation of self-defining or solitary witches, who in a more individualistic age could now dispense with the collective life of a coven and acquire the basic tenets of Wicca without the need for personal contact or initiation.[110] In so doing, Wicca moved away from its origins as a mystery religion and into the public sphere, its cause advanced by the proliferation of guides that owed their inspiration, in all or in part, to Valiente's work. Her *Rebirth of Witchcraft,* published in 1989, provided a personal, narrative history of modern Pagan witchcraft that cast Gardner as an essentially benign figure, though capable of acts of duplicity and intrinsically flawed through his insatiable publicity seeking. It also engaged in a thoughtful and constructive manner with the 'impulse of feminist witchcraft', emanating from the United States in the 1970s–80s, and linked its influence to fresh developments within British Wicca, accepting 'that there is a case for mystery and magic that is exclusive to women'.[111] In acknowledging the impact of feminist activism and the potentialities inherent in Dianic witchcraft, Valiente was operating within Gardner's own boundaries of 'pragmatic realism' and ongoing creative relationship with new source materials and cultural influences, which sought to prioritise engagement and synthesis over adherence to fixed form or dogma.[112] Indeed, part of Wicca's growing appeal lay in its mutability and often prescient agility in anticipating and assimilating new and sometimes challenging forces, whether concerning gender, ecology, or the proliferation of nuclear weapons.[113]

Ray Bone (1911–2001) ran one of the most prominent, productive, and long-lived covens to emerge in the 1960s, becoming a pivotal point of contact for those interested in engagement with Gardnerian witchcraft through her frequent public talks, radio interviews, and newspaper articles in which she promoted Gardner's vision of witchcraft as a beneficent religion, far removed from any taint of devilry and Satanism. In a similar fashion, Lois Bourne (b.1928) ran her own successful coven and penned three accounts charting her magical journey

---

[110] D. Valiente, *Witchcraft for Tomorrow,* pp. 155–194.
[111] D. Valiente, *The Rebirth of Magic*, (London: Robert Hale, 1989 rpt. 2007), pp. 191, 195.
[112] J. Pearson, 'Assumed Affinities: Wicca and the New Age', in J. Pearson, R. H. Roberts & G. Samuel (eds.), *Nature Religion Today: Paganism in the Modern World*, (Edinburgh: Edinburgh University Press, 1998), p. 47.
[113] S. M. Pike, '"Wild Nature" and the Lure of the Past: The Legacy of Romanticism among Young Pagan Environmentalists', in Feraro & Doyle White (eds.), *Magic and Modern Witchery in the Modern West,* pp. 131–152; M. Adler, *Drawing down the Moon: Witches, Druids, Goddess-Worshippers, and Other Pagans in America Today*, revised ed., (New York: Penguin, 1979 rpt. 1997), pp. 176–229.

through a 'pagan religion reborn'. Of these, *Dancing with Witches*, first published in 1998, provides a touching and unembellished account of her friendship with Gerald Gardner over the last six years of his life. Despite odd lapses of memory over names (which might have originated from no more than the desire to protect the identities and privacy of individuals), it is factual, packed full of biographical detail, and free from any attempt at self-aggrandisement. Furthermore, it is profoundly optimistic in tone, contrasting Gardner's pessimism over the survival of Wicca with its remarkable growth and cultural pull in the years after his death. 'The old gods are stirring,' she writes in way of a conclusion, 'so that we recognise' in our attitude to the planet's ecology 'that the natural world and the divine world are one.'[114]

Patricia Crowther's (b.1927) quiet, patient, and often unglamorous work, undertaken over more than five decades, attempted to explain the nature of revived witchcraft to audiences wherever they could be found. This involved speaking engagements at university debating societies, meetings of the Women's Institute, Conservative Party socials, local radio and television features, and in village halls up and down the land. These talks, together with her frequent columns and letters to the local and national press, did much to propagate Gardner's vision of witchcraft and to guarantee the continuance of a measure of religious toleration, helping to ensure that the witchcraft statutes were not reimposed as a response to periodic spasms of moral panic and fears of Satanic conspiracies. Possessing beauty, poise, and a fierce intelligence, she appeared the very archetype of the Gardnerian witch. Her first book, *The Witches Speak*, co-authored with her husband, Arnold, set the pattern to be followed by later Wiccan writers (including Doreen Valiente, Lois Bourne, and Stewart and Janet Farrar) in providing an introduction to Wicca, together with an overview of its rites, calendar, practices, and folkloric customs. It was concise, measured, and entertaining, rattling through themes drawn from popular history, drawing clear distinctions between spiritualism and witchcraft, and reprising Gardner's core teachings. Witches appeared as being inquisitive, well-read, philanthropic, and diametrically opposed to any form of necromancy or demonic magic. Theirs was (and still is, claimed the Crowthers) a matriarchal, fertility religion with the 'female [being] the most important sex in the old religion'. The account contained an incipient, though perhaps unintended, radicalism within its pages. A sense of feminism, a rejection of all forms of racism at home and abroad, and a strong sense of animal rights stemming from Patricia Crowther's lifelong engagement with the cause, were all new to Wicca. If the breakthrough of Wicca in North America was in large measure enabled by

---

[114] Bourne, *Dancing with Witches*, p. 222.

its appeal to the nascent women's and environmental movements – as the religious informed the political – then, in opening the Craft to these themes, the Crowthers were instrumental in the process.

Gardner's immediate heir, and chief beneficiary of his will, was Monique Wilson (c.1923 or 1928–82). A comparatively recent initiate, she had come to Gardner's attention during a crisis within the small network of Scottish covens, when a High Priest had attempted to exert his authority as Gardner's deputy and laid claim to the title of 'Chief Witch of Scotland'. Faced with this challenge, Gardner had shown no hesitation in striking fast, humbling a would-be patriarchal rival and elevating Wilson, as a High Priestess, in his stead. Thereafter, during the last years of his life, Gardner became increasingly close to the whole Wilson family and, in a move that came as a bolt from the blue to his established inner circle, hastily revised his will in the days before his death, bequeathing to Monique the greater part of his fortune, his home in Castletown, his literary estate and the entire contents of his museum. The Manx museum now had a female witch to celebrate and altered its imagery accordingly, while the Wilsons republished Gardner's books on witchcraft and began a media offensive. The difficulty was that in facing down the aspiring 'Chief Witch', Monique had prevailed upon Gardner to grant her the title of 'Queen of the Witches'. Fully cognisant of the damage that this move would do to his relationship with his other High Priestesses, Gardner (who compartmentalised his life, dealings and personal relationships) kept it secret from his other confidants, and rationalised it as being no more than a courtesy title. However, following Gardner's death, Monique's attempt to exert authority over the entire Wiccan community as *the* Witch Queen spectacularly backfired and drew nothing but criticism down upon her from the other High Priestesses. It struck at the egalitarian grain of Gardner's teachings and the view that while one might write, create, and argue within the Craft, there was no 'goddess-given' insight over and above that of any other witch. Aside from polarising opinion against her, the only tangible result of this power-play was its impact upon the fledgling culture of Wicca in the United States, whereby High Priests and Priestesses adopted ever more high-flown titles (such as 'Duke', 'Count', and 'Lady') and in Britain, where Alex Sanders, an aspiring young ceremonial magician, and one-time spiritualist medium, chose to press his claim as 'King of the Witches' at the height of the 1960s counterculture.

Another difficulty lay in the fact that, unlike Patricia Crowther, Doreen Valiente, and Lois Bourne: Monique Wilson was not a writer. A lengthy BBC interview recorded in the mid-1960s, reveals her to be well versed in Gardner's writings and utterly sincere in her beliefs, but subject to being talked over by her husband at key points.[115] Though gifted in a ritual setting and successful as a teacher (implanting Wicca in North America through the Bucklands) she was far from being an innovator and was painfully exposed when asked to explain the ideas and allusions contained within Gardner's books that neither she nor her husband fully understood. Politically reactionary, if socially liberal, she was ill-suited to capitalising upon Wicca's feminist and anti-authoritarian appeal. Yet, it was her courting of the press that ultimately destroyed her. In this, we can see the double standards employed by the tabloids in their treatment of her, as compared to Gardner: with her sex and sexuality used, with heavy doses of innuendo to suggest chthonic threat, diabolism, and deviancy. With her own network of covens that had ranged from Scotland and the North of England to the East Coast of America, crumbling and the museum haemorrhaging money as the result of neglect and mismanagement, the sale of Gardner's archives and collections was concluded, in 1973, with the *Ripley's Believe It or Not* chain. The departure of the Wilsons to start a new life as bar owners in a Spanish seaside resort, coupled with the swiftness and secrecy of the museum's sale, seemed to make Wicca vanish, almost overnight, from the Isle of Man, while the corporation's ownership of his personal documents and papers effectively precluded further serious attempts to research his life and work through primary sources.[116] Herein lies a major reason for Gardner's crisis of visibility within the history of Wicca, from the 1970s to the 1980s, enabling his detractors to hold the field, without challenge.

However, even if Gardner had attempted, in his final years, to fast-track initiates through the Craft (often whisking them through all three degrees within a matter of days), he was remarkably successful (whether by discernment or by sheer luck) in training and inspiring a remarkable group of women to follow his precepts and to devote the rest of their lives to promoting and advancing the interpretative trail that he had blazed. If he mis-stepped with Monique Wilson, then he struck a seam of pure gold with Ray Bone, Lois Pearson, and Patricia Crowther. Even Doreen Valiente, who broke with him in 1957, spent the rest of her career working and reworking the concept of Wicca that he had outlined. Furthermore, there was never a hint of predation in these relationships. His High Priestesses held him in fond regard, with Lois Bourne writing of him as 'a treasured, valued and trusted' friend, and 'a very gentle person and very generous in his estimate of other people'; and with Doreen Valiente describing him as 'a great person' who 'did great work in bringing back the Old Religion to

---

[115] Museum of Witchcraft & Magic, Boscastle, 'Interview with Charles [sic – actually Campbell] & Monique Wilson', c.1965, item no.3821.

[116] J. H. Steele, *Souvenir Booklet: Dr. Gardner's Museum of . . . Magic and Superstition*, (San Francisco: Ripley's Believe It or Not!, 1976), pp. 6, 23–24, 26–27, 42, 44–45.

many people' and as 'a man utterly without malice', who 'would have literally shared his last crust with his worst enemy'.[117] Patricia Crowther remembered him 'as an individual of great intelligence and charm', who had no equal terms of his kindness and his essential curiosity, and who appeared as 'the Mercurial Herald of the Old Religion'.[118] Against such reminiscences could, of course, be set the withering scorn of Olive Parsons, but, although her testimony was bought and paid for by a man who hated and sought to destroy him, Gardner emerges from her account as no more than a slightly eccentric old man and as a model of gentlemanly restraint when it came to dealing with those who wished to lay him low.[119] Ironically, the Gardnerian 'Witch Cult' had very little of the sense of the cultic, in its modern pejorative sense and it strangely fitting that this term – harking back to the mysteries of Egyptian and Classical Greek religion – was bestowed by a First Wave feminist: Margaret Murray.

By the time of the advent of the Second Wave of feminism, the witch could be 'all-woman' and her Craft described, by a North American situationist group in 1968, as being the sum of:

> theatre, revolution, magic, terror, joy, garlic flowers, spells. It's an awareness that witches and gypsies were the original guerrillas and resistance fighters against oppression – particularly the oppression of women – down through the ages. Witches have always been women who dared to be . . . courageous, aggressive, intelligent, nonconformist, explorative, curious, independent, sexually liberated, revolutionary.[120]

This heady mix of the creative and the romantic, alongside hard-headed rallying calls to political activism, was very much in the spirit of 'the year of the barricades' and laid claim to the witch as an emblematic figure and role model for women who sought to redefine and reclaim their societal position. Key to this process in the writings of Zsuzsanna Budapest (aka Zsuzsanna Emese Mokcsay b.1940) and Starhawk (aka Miriam Simos b.1951) was the primacy of the mother goddess and the re-sacralisation of the female as both a reflection and centring of the divine. This elevated the goddess, placed marked accent upon 'the personal as political' and retained both Wicca's supportive

---

[117] Bourne, *Dancing with Witches*, pp. 19, 33; Valiente, *The Rebirth of Witchcraft*, p. 80; D. Valiente, *An ABC of Witchcraft Past & Present*, (London: Robert Hale, 1973 rpt.1994), pp. 157–158.

[118] P. Crowther, *From Stagecraft to Witchcraft. The Early Years of a High Priestess*, (Milverton, Somerset: Capall Bann, 2002), p. 142; P. Crowther, *Lid Off the Cauldron. A Handbook for Witches*, (London: Frederick Muller Ltd., 1981), p. 33.

[119] 'Rex Nemorensis' (aka C. Cardell), *Witch*, copy of Gardner's letter on an unnumbered page between pp. 9–10; and pp. 53–54.

[120] WITCH Manifesto quoted in: M. Adler, *Drawing Down the Moon. Witches, Druids, Goddess-Worshippers, and Other Pagans in America Today*, p. 179.

historical imagination and matrilineal structure, while dispensing with the Horned God, the sense of sexual polarity, and initiatory covens which had all been hallmarks of Gardnerian Wicca. In the case of Budapest, male agency was entirely excluded from her new Dianic branch of witchcraft, and it might be argued that, within a US context, the pantheon was pruned back in order to celebrate the mother goddess (or sometimes Gaia) in a manner more immediately appreciable to a monotheistic culture, where the gender of the godhead had been switched and the attributes of the Abrahamic God negated through their feminine, polar opposites.

Central to Starhawk's work was the idea that religious 'truths' might be expressed through the mythopoetic rather than the philosophical and that witchcraft had 'always' been primarily a religion of poetry as opposed to theology. Indeed, the strength of her best-selling, *The Spiral Dance*, published in 1979, lay in large measure through the quality of her charms, chants, and rites, which captivated and inspired a whole new generation of witches through their beauty. They built a coherent picture of ritual practice and spellcraft, rooted in the seasonal change of the wheel of the year, that owed its essential form and expression to Gardner's Wicca, but which added a freshness of language and permitted the reader to grasp, quickly, easily, and independently, the core rites and guiding principles of a fully revived witchcraft.[121]

Her witches were the political rebels and eco-campaigners *par excellence*, who had fought and suffered during the European witch-hunts on account of their opposition to the great expropriation of common land by the wealthy.[122] Just as significant, her willingness to accept the nature and significance of myth within religion permitted a view of witchcraft as being 'eternally reinvented, changing, growing, alive' because of the Goddess' presence with it. This, perhaps more than anything else, allowed Wicca to survive the successive hammer-blows of the 1980s–90s, when many of its founding myths, rooted in Margaret Murray's work and Gardner's own imaginative rendering of history, were being stripped away one-by-one and it was no longer tenable to argue that witchcraft was either hereditary or rooted within Stone Age survivals. Starhawk's work effectively represented its own 'second wave' of a witchcraft revival, which acknowledged fresh societal developments that had taken place since the late 1950s and early 1960s, and which permitted solitary alongside formal, coven-based witchcraft, the gradual dropping of the idea of the 'High' priestess or priest within her expression of the Craft, the

---

[121] Starhawk, *The Spiral Dance: A Rebirth of the Ancient Religion of the Great Goddess*, revised ed., (New York: HarperSanFrancisco, 1979 rpt. 1989), pp. 2–3.

[122] Starhawk, *Dreaming the Dark: Magic, Sex & Politics*, (Boston: Beacon Press, 1982), pp. 189–199.

further enhancement and celebration of the role of women, and a far more open attitude towards homosexuality within Wicca. As such, it was far better equipped to remain relevant and to grow during very different times.

Yet, in comparison to Gardner's overwhelming sense of optimism, there was a growing sense of bleakness in Starhawk's work. The world was finite, its resources failing due to exploitation. The witches were witnessing a planet in its death throes and Wicca as a fertility religion shifted its focus, accordingly. The act of struggle and personal empowerment replaced Gardner's concept of pleasure and happiness; and humanity was required to act to save the natural world, rather than nature acting as the solace and provider for humanity. It might be argued that these developments were natural responses to environmental and nuclear threats, channelling a pessimism that stemmed from the electoral success of the political Right, on both sides of the Atlantic, in the 1980s, and the impact of the economic 'shock doctrine' of neoliberalism. Yet Gardner wrote in similarly threatening times, at the outset of the Cold War, and in a climate of stifling political and moral reaction, under the Eden, Macmillan, and Douglas Hume governments. He was equally opposed to nuclear weapons, chafing against their existence as early as 1949, but (aside from the foundational myth of 'the cone of power') had never seen Wicca as a means to reshape the world.[123] The escalating sense of rage, loss, and intrinsic struggle channelled through Wicca, from the late 1970s, was alien to him. However, we should remember as a privileged man, he had never had to experience an alienation created by fundamental gender inequality and had never had to fight to reclaim control of his own body and reproductive rights in the manner of Second Wave feminists.

In the UK, Monica Sjöö (1938–2005), as both painter and author, combined art with radical political activism and a goddess-based feminism, honouring the 'Great Cosmic Mother'. In doing so, she elicited support from Doreen Valiente in her stands against nuclear weapons and patriarchal forms within both witchcraft and the wider New Age movement.[124] Influenced by Robert Graves' *White Goddess* and by pilgrimages to Silbury Hill and the Avebury Stone Circle, Sjöö showcased her art in pioneering women-only shows, and explored both the Celtic and Nordic traditions through an avowedly feminist lens. Hers was a modern Paganism shaped by sit-ins, protests, situationist happenings, peace camps, and free festivals, where Nordic trolls were the distant echoes of a lost moon worshipping people; where Huldra walked the forests by night; and where

---

[123] Gardner, *High Magic's Aid*, p. 211.

[124] S. Feraro, 'Playing the Pipes of PAN: Pagans Against Nukes and the Linking oof Wicca-Derived Paganism with Ecofeminism in Britain, 1980-1990', in S. Feraro & E. Doyle White (eds.), *Magic and Witchery in the Modern West* (Eastbourne: Palgrave Macmillan, 2019), p. 54.

Rhiannon, Brigid, and Cerridwen stood guardian to the land and mourned at its rape through man's building of nuclear bunkers and motorway extensions.

Vivianne Crowley's enormously influential book on *Wicca*, first published in 1989, drew upon her experiences in covens descended from both Ray Bone and Alex Sanders, and her synthesis of differing traditions, welcoming of difference, and generosity of spirit charted a way through the sectarian squabbles that had divided the Gardnerian and Alexandrian lines of witchcraft in the 1980s. Gardner's foundational story of Wicca was accepted at face value (which was understandable a decade before the publication of *The Triumph of the Moon*), and Gardner, himself, was credited with transforming Wicca 'from a religion of the past, into a religion for the future'.[125] For once, a 'how to' guide actually delivered on its promises, with thematic chapters building a sense of Wicca's culture and practice, detailing rituals, initiatory steps, and points of departure. Elements of Dion Fortune's practice stood alongside concepts harking back to the Order of the Golden Dawn, while the influence of Eastern esoteric religion was introduced through a discussion of opening and closing the chakras. After all, as Crowley pointed out, Gardner original's group had been adept at the cross-fertilisation of ideas and traditions, being 'familiar with the Classical Pagan Mysteries, ritual magic, and Paganism of Greece and Rome, and ... had a knowledge of Eastern traditions of Goddess worship and the use of etheric energy'.[126] However, while Gardner had touched upon Jungian analysis of mythos and archetype, Crowley placed it at the centre of her work, viewing revived Pagan witchcraft through his interpretative lens. If Gardner had sought to create a religion around Margaret Murray's historical imagination, then Crowley reforged Wicca as an expression of Gustav Jung's studies in psychiatry and mysticism. This had the effect of giving Wicca, which had always been derided by the academic, and theocratic, mainstream as being facile and lacking in a philosophy of religion, a coherence, a language, and an interpretive framework that accentuated its rationalism to the outside world while providing a clearer rationale for its beliefs and practices to its adherents. Lacking the political militancy and class consciousness that animated Starhawk and Sjöö, Crowley's work accepted the same feminist critique of society and similarly relegated the Horned God (dominant in Murray and an equal partner in Gardner) to the background. Building upon Budapest's ideas, there was a universal goddess, now explicitly identified as Gaia, 'the Earth itself', who was immanent and in-dwelling in all of creation, possessing three aspects: as Virgin, Mother, and Hag.[127] Such a division neatly appropriated for Wicca ideas that had been

---

[125] V. Crowley, *Wicca: A Comprehensive Guide to the Old Religion in the Modern World*, (London: Element / HarperCollins, 1989 rpt. 2003), p. 33.
[126] Crowley, *Wicca*. [127] Crowley, *Wicca*, p. 137.

crystallising in the North American New Age and radical feminist movements since the early 1970s, though to an outsider it might seem to replicate the Christian trinity, with a tripartite goddess as opposed to a god. It certainly marked a significant departure from Gardner's original vision of gendered polarity as being the driving force behind all creation, and the multiplicity of different, and individualistic, expressions of the divine through a pantheon of gods and goddesses. Wicca was suddenly more appreciable and formal, but less wildly eclectic. What did remain constant was the sense within Pagan witchcraft that 'It is woman who has the ultimate power'.[128]

By the turn of the millennium, Wicca was becoming increasingly diverse, diffuse, and feminised, In this way, its ongoing development resembled that of the oak tree which, through its growth, bears little superficial likeness to the acorn from which it grew, yet it still retain its same nature, genetic potential, substance, and life force. Thus, there was a witchcraft to suit everybody: whether solitary or group practitioners; 'traditional', Northern (i.e. Norse); Dianic, Hekatean, queer, non-binary, inclusive, Heathen, Alexandrian, or Gardnerian.

The Wicca (or Wica) as understood by Gardner as a group designation of wise folk had long since been replaced by its popular connotation as a blanket term for a revived form of Pagan witchcraft. His achievement in both areas was to make paganism synonymous with witchcraft in a manner that historically it had never been and by removing Satan and devil worship from its cosmology and practice. In wrenching away the interpolation of demonic forces by the Patristic Fathers from the surviving kernel of Classical religion, Gardner had, literally and metaphorically, cleansed the altars of paganism and permitted their votive fires to be re-lit. This was a – and perhaps even *the* – vital development in enabling Wicca to become a feminist, and feminised religion. If the witch could not be owned as a positive role model and an archetype of womanhood; if she remained the product of absolute poverty and irrational superstition, mired in allegations of child murder, ignorance, and utter malignity; then there was little hope for her celebration and advancement as the 'all woman' and heartbeat of the earth. Gardner was able to rehabilitate her figure, stressing aspects of healing, intelligence, and intuition within her make-up, while retaining the certain edginess that the term 'witch' conveys. If he had wanted it otherwise, then 'Pagan' would have sufficed and Wicca might have developed along lines already explored by Edward Carpenter and the circle around Rupert Brooke.[129]

---

[128] Crowley, *Wicca*, p. 146.

[129] S. Rowbotham, *Edward Carpenter: A Life of Liberty and Love*, (London: Verso, 2008 rpt. 2009), pp. 253, 297–298, 408–410; P. Delaney, *The Neo-Pagans. Friendship and Love in the Rupert Brooke Circle*, (London: Macmillan, 1987), pp. 39–43, 66, 72, 101.

However, as Starhawk perceptively noted: 'the names that carry power, often sound simple, childish or threatening ... the concept of the Witch goes against the grain of the culture of estrangement. It *should* rub us the wrong way'.[130] The use of the word was, at once, an act of reclamation and affirmation. As such, it stands as one of Gerald Gardner's greatest, though largely unintended, triumphs.

7 The World: The Achievement of Modern Paganism

The spaces between matter. Wicca is a liminal religion. It was never intended, as Gardner pointed out, to be 'for everyone'. It did not set out to proselytise or to convert. Its mantra, 'once a witch, always a witch' stressed that the assumption of witchcraft was a form of coming home, of self-realisation, or reconnection with a past life. The mysteries sat at its epicentre, the source of inquiry, expression, revelation, and creation; but understood as being ultimately beyond the bounds of human cognition and incapable of reduction to formulas, balance sheets, and the realms of doctrine. Gardner saw it operating as a function of group egregore, to facilitate the seizure of its High Priestesses and, to a lesser degree, Priests by the divinities, and to achieve a wider communion with the gods through techniques of consciousness raising through religious ecstasy, as opposed to simple frenzy.

Significantly, the synthesised Pagan religion that Gardner forged cast no shadow of Christianity. His was not a demon-haunted world, with life as a mere passage between judgments to be saved or damned. Instead, rather like Kipling's Kimball O' Hara, he was exceptionally sensitive and receptive to the impressions made upon him through his contacts with the religious practices of the East, keen to learn, non-judgemental, and fascinated by their differences and vibrancy. Like 'Kim', he operated on the margins of colonialism, in pursuit of its vital, but largely disreputable, interests. He differed only in the fact that he had no single teacher and was compelled to become his own holy man. Distanced from Europe, in terms of both geography and outlook, he was able to shed the leaden mantle of Western Christianity in a manner that was radically new and unattainable for other occultists. John Dee had sought to communicate with angels within a monotheistic universe; MacGregor Matthews had steeped himself in a high magic that grew out of an Abrahamic tradition; Crowley claimed the Devil as anti-hero; and Dion Fortune sought a mystical union through her magic between Jesus and the Rosy Cross; while Alex Sanders was entranced by the power of Roman Catholic ritual, vestments, and authority. All too often, the feminist witches of the 1970s–80s sought to reframe Wicca as

---
[130] Starhawk, *Dreaming the Dark,* p. 25.

the negation of Christianity, occluding pantheism, replacing one monotheism (and trinity) with another and creating a language and an imagery that frequently appeared as the shadow to evangelical Christianity and the Home Church movement. Gardner sidestepped all of this. Through his constant revision of the *Book of Shadows*, he continued his attempts to find a 'right fit' and feel for his magic that gradually stripped away the Abrahamic influences found in the *Key of Solomon*, and other early modern grimoires, to achieve what he felt to be a Pagan expression through the interplay of ritual and language. He removed the binary opposites (the sense of the Manichean divide between 'good' and 'evil') from his religious practice, emphasising instead the need for balance between the light and the dark within the world. As a consequence, he both excluded the possibility of maleficia from Wicca and brought its spirit closer to that of Classical paganism.

Gardner understood the gulf of 1,600 years that separated the last mystery religions of Antiquity from his own age. We are not them; they are not us. The gaps in the historical record occasioned by the imposition of one religious culture over another (starting with the concept of a 'year zero' in human affairs with the birth of Jesus) were simply unbridgeable. Lacking access to major research libraries, he sought clues and inspiration wherever he could, demonstrating a magpie-like ability to appropriate ideas and themes from an eclectic range of source materials that encompassed literature, popular history and science, archaeology and anthropology. His lack of formal education, allied to the sense of his cheerful anarchism, ensured that he was wary of systems (and system building), whether expressed on a societal or theocratic level. Wicca was to be a humanist religion, lived in the moment, with the aim of finding fulfilment through life as opposed to death. Moreover, by the very nature of its cross-cultural synchronicities and syntheses, it was a religion of tolerance: a tolerance of difference, of other peoples, and other belief systems. The universalist message of Wicca was embodied in its idea of a Stone Age fertility cult that had once been common to all. Long before 'year zero', the coming of western civilisation, and totalitarian faiths, there *had* – he argued – to have been other rougher, yet kindlier religions based in the magics of the tribe, that were accessible and experienced by all. It was precisely expressions of animism and the spirit world that he had immersed himself within during his time in Borneo, Burma, and Malaysia. These were relevant and vibrant belief systems that still survived and even flourished. It was not entirely unreasonable for Gardner to have sought for the echoes of their practices in a British context.

If it was tolerant, then Wicca was also permissive. It was intended to release, rather than constrain, human potential. As such, it could offer the promise of transgressive hedonism, but, more importantly, it could equally offer self-fulfilment and self-realisation. Without this sense of the unbridled creative impulse, and the celebration of creativity as a divine act, it is nothing. Its only prohibitions are against harming others; seeking financial gain for the practice of its art; and 'oath breaking' in revealing its inner-most mysteries to the uninitiated. In this way, it aimed to preserve its links to the cultic practices and mystery religions of the Graeco-Roman World (of Isis, Demeter, Dionysus, and Mithras) but was also the product of Renaissance humanism and the anthropomorphic drive of the European Enlightenment. Again, it is the sense of liminality and paradox that has permitted its survival and sustenance. For, whether it likes it or not, Wicca lives in a constant state of tension with the values, social attitudes, and legal preconditions forged by the Enlightenment. If the majority of modern Europeans were not possessed of a rationalist world view that discounted the efficacy of magic and the immanence of religion, then witchcraft would, once again, be something to be feared and, ultimately, extirpated. In this manner, the disbelief of the mainstream enabled toleration of belief at the margins. Gardner understood this dilemma very well, and his career and packaging of Wicca were calculated in such a way as to walk the tightrope, publicising the reality of a benign form of natural magic, without occasioning a renewed form of repression. If modern Pagans have flirted with post-modernity and excoriated Western rationalism and scientific method, then the blunt – if not yet brutal – reality is that Wicca requires the survival of Enlightenment thought within wider society and its governance to guarantee its continuing toleration and practice. Similarly, revived Paganism's reverence of nature and concern for animal rights is a product of enlightened modernity and stands in marked opposition to Classical paganism's desire to propitiate the natural world and to offer blood sacrifices.

The need for the Enlightenment to act as bulwark against rising fundamentalisms is doubly important as Wicca lacks a resistance doctrine. Far from a religion of conquest, institutional power, or suffering, it remains largely underground and comparatively unnoticed. Gardner's own museum fell victim to the evangelical religious reaction that underpinned Ronald Reagan's United States, in the 1980s, closed down, packed away, and sold off piecemeal by the *Ripley's* corporation that found itself, suddenly, out-of-step with an increasingly conservative society, fearful of its ownership and display of 'Satanic' artefacts. A decade later, the same moral panic crossed the Atlantic Ocean and saw children removed from their parents by social workers, with local politicians and liberal newspaper journalists, as well as Christian fundamentalists, equating witchcraft with Satanic child abuse. It took exceptional individual and professional courage, and a protracted public campaign on the part of the Pagan

Federation, to dispel the unfounded allegations and achieve a measure of restorative justice.[131] Though this existential threat did act as a centrifuge, the increasing diversity of practice and individualisation of belief served to atomise the Pagan community once the immediate danger had passed. With families and livelihoods threatened, it was not surprising that the lineages descending from Gardner's original covens tended to prefer quiet anonymity and to bitterly resent any attempts to 'out' their membership by journalists or apostates intent on creating a media sensation. Gardner, who had long campaigned for the repeal of the Witchcraft Act of 1736, was fully aware of the forces ranged against him and of the fragility of Wicca's new-found freedoms. As such, he attempted to thread a vein of steel through its early development, emphasising its 'martyrs', redeploying Matilda Joslyn Gage's dystopian idea of 'the burning times', and evoking the witch as outlaw of the greenwood and tribune of the people. Gardner's fascination with weaponry was more than enough to suggest that self-defence and the act of possession of multiple bladed weapons meant that Wicca did not, necessarily, have to be passive or pacific.

It should be apparent that Gardner was not simply engaged in fabricating a new religion. Instead, he was able to channel countercultural themes, societal shifts, and religious and magical themes that had been germinating since the Romantic Revival of the nineteenth century and create for them a unifying form of expression and relevance. As an autodidact and outsider, hampered by a lack of academic education and influential connections, it has seemed incongruous that the modern Pagan revival flourished under his hand, and not that of those (such as Rupert Brooke, Edward Carpenter, Robert Graves, or even Aleister Crowley) whose poetry and prose possessed greater beauty, substance, and clarity. Equally out-of-kilter is his gender. It is an uncomfortable fact that the well-spring of feminist witchcraft was a man, rather than a woman such as Dion Fortune, Margaret Murray, or Doreen Valiente. Consequently, Gerald Gardner has been the subject of condescension and historical revisionism. He did not fit the available paradigms, but then, in his own terms, what messenger of the gods ever did? For better or for worse, Wicca was fashioned according to his own interests and priorities and has, against all expectations, flourished and grown.

Gardner succeeded where it mattered to him most: in the establishment and continuance of a viable form of Pagan witchcraft. He left behind him, at most, a few hundred adherents mainly in the UK. Today, British and Irish witches descended from Gardner's direct line probably number somewhere in the low thousands, with approximately 13,000 individuals self-defining as Wiccans in

---

[131] Hutton, *Triumph of the Moon,* pp. 385–386, 389. See also: A. Boyd, *Blasphemous Rumours: Is Satanic Ritual Abuse Fact or Fantasy? An Investigation*, (London: Fount / HarperCollins, 1995).

the 2021 UK Census. Though methods of religious identification are hampered by the construction of the survey (for instance, 'No Religion' covers a whole range of positions from atheist to those who would prefer privacy in matters of belief), what is significant are the strong numerical presence of wider cross-fertilising groups who have identified as Pagans (74,000), Shamans (8,000), Heathens (4,722), and Druids (2,489), and whose numbers have risen steadily, if not dramatically, since the 1990s. As such, a revived Paganism stands as a significant religious impulse that dwarfs, in numerical terms, new religious forms such as Scientology and Hare Krishna, and ancient faiths such as Jainism and Zoroastrianism.[132] This alone is suggestive that Wicca is deserving of greater respect and attention than it has been often accorded on a societal and theological level, as an entirely valid and viable comparative religion, complete with its own history, mythos, and beliefs. Although similarly fraught with interpretative difficulty (as the Religious Identification Survey continually altered its definitions and reporting; and Christian fundamentalists have been keen to talk-up its 'threat' without offering much in the way of substantive data), Paganism appears to have been similarly experiencing small, but consistent, growth in the United States since the 1990s. It seems fair to agree with the findings of the Pew Institute Religious Landscape Study, in 2014, that at 0.03 per cent of the population defining as either Pagan or Wiccan, a revived witchcraft stands parallel to small Protestant dominations, such as the Quakers or Congregational Churches, who draw their inspiration from the religious ferment of the 1640s–60s.[133] Within this context, Wicca would seem to be a durable system, possessed of a cultural relevance that outweighs its numerical strength, and largely insulated from the debunking of many of its founding myths since the 1990s.

That it has endured as a mutable and vital force owes much to the flexibility of approach, sense of tolerance, and potent religious imagination of Gerald Gardner. The synthesis he achieved, between old and new nature religions; of high and low magical traditions; and of experiential occult practice with a profoundly humanistic telos; permitted the re-enchantment of the landscape, the re-sacralisation of the body, and the celebration of human potentialities and creativity as aspects of, and tributes to, the divine. His gods could as easily be present among the woodsmoke and seances of the Dyaks, in Borneo, as they could among the overgrown sanctuaries of the Classical world, among the hoarfrosts in the New Forest, or in the sunrise catching the Meayall Stone Circle on the Isle of Man. If we have dispensed with the Gardner of popular

---

[132] See the analysis of the 2021 Census by the President of the Pagan Federation: www.paganfed.org/census-2021-results/.

[133] https://wildhunt.org/2019/01/estimating-growing-number-of-us-pagans.html.

myth, the fusty, nervous, and duplicitous civil servant, cloaked in the mores of empire and establishment, then, we are beholden to recognise both his brilliance and bravura; his essential radicalism in the ability to inhabit and to create from the margins; and his essential generosity of spirit – that most intangible and all-too-often decried quality – that imbued Wicca with, perhaps, its greatest quality of a vision that owned mutability and diversity.

His confidants recalled the surety of his art within the Circle, his possession of quiet majesty, his stillness and sense of awe when faced with what he took to be divine, channelling the will of the gods and embracing the divine. Such moments are fleeting and entirely subjective yet combine to form the essence of Wicca. Accept them or dismiss them; they – as opposed to exercises in form criticism – are the key to its lasting appeal and understanding. Had Gardner pursued a quiet retirement or died before the publication of *Witchcraft Today,* then he would have passed largely without notice, and it is likely that Paganism would have remained a fringe interest and that witchcraft, separated from it, would have remained a diabolical and detested art. As it was, the remarkable ferment of activity and ideas that marked the last twenty-five years of his life established Wicca as his own alchemical wedding between the paganism of the Classical and developing worlds and the healing, feminised witchcraft of the future. As such, it was fitting testament to his 'potent art ... this rough magic'.[134]

---

[134] Shakespeare, *The Tempest,* Act V Scene 1.

Bibliography

Adler, M., *Drawing down the Moon: Witches, Druids, Goddess-Worshippers, and Other Pagans in America Today*, revised & expanded edition, (New York: Penguin / Arkana, 1979 rpt. 1997).

Baker, A. R., 'The Scholar the Builders Rejected – The Life & Work of J.S.M. Ward', *Ars Quatuor Coronatorum: Being the Proceedings of Quator Coronati Lodge No. 2076*, Vol. 116, (October 2004), pp.127–192.

Berger, H. A., (ed.), *Witchcraft and Magic: Contemporary North America*, (Philadelphia: University of Philadelphia Press, 2005).

Bourne, L., *Dancing with Witches*, (London: Robert Hale, 1998 rpt. 2006).

Bracelin, J., *Gerald Gardner: Witch*, (London: The Octagon Press, 1960).

Buckland, R., *Witchcraft from the Inside*, 3rd ed., (St. Paul: Llewellyn Publications, 1971 rpt. 1996).

Callow, J., 'New Magic at the Old Mill: Gerald Gardner, the Manx Museum of Witchcraft & the Fashioning of the Wica', *Isle of Man Studies. Proceedings of the Isle of Man Natural History and Antiquarian Society*, Vol. XVI (2019), pp. 93–124.

Callow, J., *Prospero's Isle: Gerald Gardner and Witchcraft on the Isle of Man*, (London: Rose Ankh, 2025).

Clifton, C. S., *Her Hidden Children: The Rise of Wicca and Paganism in America*, (Oxford: AltaMira Press, 2006).

Crowley, V., *Wicca: A Comprehensive Guide to the Old Religion in the Modern World*, (London: HarperCollins, 1989 rpt. 2003).

Crowther, A, & Crowther, P., *The Witches Speak*, (Douglas: Athol, 1965).

Crowther, P., *Lid Off the Cauldron: A Handbook for Witches*, (London: Frederick Muller Ltd., 1981).

Doyle White, E., *Wicca: History, Belief, and Community in Modern Pagan Witchcraft*, (Brighton: Sussex Academic Press, 2016).

Feraro, S., & Doyle White, E., (eds.), *Magic and Witchery in the Modern West: Celebrating the Twentieth Anniversary of the Triumph of the Moon*, (Eastbourne: Palgrave Macmillan, 2019).

Gardner, G. B., *A Goddess Arrives*, (London: Arthur H. Stockwell Ltd., n/d. c.1939–40).

Gardner, G. B., *High Magic's Aid*, (London: Michael Houghton, 1949, rpt. Milton Keynes, Aurinia Books, 2010).

Gardner, G. B., *Keris and Other Malay Weapons*, (Singapore: Progressive, 1936).

Gardner, G. B., *The Meaning of Witchcraft*, (London: The Aquarian Press, 1959 rpt. 1971).

Gardner, G. B., *The Museum of Witchcraft and Magic: The Story of the Famous Witches Mill at Castletown, Isle of Man*, (Tunbridge Wells: Photocrom Co. Ltd., n/d c.1958).

Gardner, G. B., *Witchcraft Today*, (London: Rider, 1954 rpt. 1956).

Gardner, G. B., 'Witchcraft . . . In the Isle of Man', *New Dimensions*, Vol.1 no.6, (February– March 1964), pp. 6–11

Graves, R., *The Crane Bag and Other Disputed Subjects*, (London: Cassell, 1969).

Heselton, P., *Doreen Valiente: Witch*, (Milton Keynes: The Doreen Valiente Foundation & the Centre for Pagan Studies, 2016).

Heselton, P., *Witchfather: A Life of Gerald Gardner, Volume 1. Into the Witch Cult*, (Loughborough: Thoth, 2012).

Heselton, P., *Witchfather: A Life of Gerald Gardner, Volume 2. From Witch Cult to Wicca*, (Loughborough: Thoth, 2012).

Howard, M., *Modern Wicca: A History from Gerald Gardner to the Present*, (Woodbury: Llewellyn, 2009).

Hughes, P., *Witchcraft*, (London: Longman, 1952 rpt. 1972).

Hutton, R., *The Pagan Religions of the Ancient British Isles: Their Nature and Legacy*, (Oxford: Blackwell, 1991 rpt. 1993).

Hutton, R., *The Triumph of the Moon: A History of Modern Pagan Witchcraft*, New ed., (Oxford: Oxford University Press, 2019).

Kaczynski, R., *Perdurabo: The Life of Aleister Crowley*, New & Expanded ed., (Berkeley: North Atlantic Books, 2010).

Kelly, A. A., *Inventing Witchcraft: A Case Study in the Creation of a New Religion*, (Loughborough: Thoth, 2007).

Lamond, F., *Fifty Years of Wicca*, (Sutton Mallet: Green Magic, 2004).

Lamond, F., *Religion without Beliefs: Essays in Pantheist Theology, Comparative Religion and Ethics*, (London: Janus, 1997 rpt. 2008).

Lewis, J. R., *Magical Religion and Modern Witchcraft*, (Albany: State University of New York Press, 1996).

Luhrmann, T. M., *Persuasions of the Witch's Craft: Ritual in Contemporary England*, (London: Picador, 1989 rpt. 1994).

Miller, S., '"Shee was the Wysest Woman in the Lande". Margaret Quane (1616)', *Isle of Man Studies: Proceedings of the Isle of Man Natural History and Historical Society*, Vol. XVIII (2023), pp. 39–52.

Murray, M. A., *The God of the Witches*, (London: Sampson Low, Marston & Co. Ltd., n/d. 1931).

Murray, M. A., *The Witch-Cult in Western Europe: A Study in Anthropology*, (Oxford: The Clarendon Press, 1921).

For EU product safety concerns, contact us at Calle de José Abascal, 56–1°, 28003 Madrid, Spain or eugpsr@cambridge.org.

www.ingramcontent.com/pod-product-compliance
Lightning Source LLC
LaVergne TN
LVHW011854060526
838200LV00054B/4333